The Eddington Memorial Lectures

FROM PARACELSUS TO NEWTON
MAGIC AND THE MAKING OF
MODERN SCIENCE

FROM PARACELSUS TO NEWTON
MAGIC AND THE MAKING OF
MODERN SCIENCE

CHARLES WEBSTER

The Eddington Memorial Lectures
Delivered at
Cambridge University
November 1980

CAMBRIDGE UNIVERSITY PRESS

Cambridge
London   New York   New Rochelle
Melbourne   Sydney

Published by the Press Syndicate of the University of Cambridge
The Pitt Building, Trumpington Street, Cambridge CB2 1RP
32 East 57th Street, New York, NY 10022, USA
296 Beaconsfield Parade, Middle Park, Melbourne 3206, Australia

First published 1982

Printed in Great Britain at the University Press, Cambridge

Library of Congress catalogue card number: 82–4586

British Library cataloguing in publication data
Webster, Charles, *1936–*
From Paracelsus to Newton: magic and the making of modern science.–
(The Eddington memorial lectures)
1. Science – History
I. Title   II. Series
509   Q125
ISBN 0 521 24919 8

DS

THE EDDINGTON LECTURESHIP

Sir Arthur Stanley Eddington, O.M., F.R.S., Plumian Professor of Astronomy at Cambridge 1913–44 was one of the greatest astronomer-mathematicians of his day. He was not only world famous as an astronomer but also as a brilliant exponent of the new developments in physics and cosmology. Two of his best-known books, *Stars and Atoms* and *The Nature of the Physical World*, were, between them, translated into twelve different languages. He was also a profound thinker; in religion and ethics as in science. His Swarthmore Lecture, *Science and the Unseen World* was deservedly one of the most valued and widely read of the series. It was produced in French, German, Danish and Dutch editions.

Eddington was a life-long Quaker; and on his death the Society of Friends, in order to provide for an annual lecture in his memory, established (as the result of a widely supported appeal for funds) a Trust with four Trustees; one each to be appointed by the Royal Society and Trinity College, Cambridge (of which Eddington was a Fellow for thirty-seven years) and two by the Society of Friends.

The scope of the lectureship, which has remained unchanged since the foundation in 1947, is as follows:

The lectures are to deal with some aspect of contemporary scientific thought considered in its bearing on the philosophy of religion or on ethics. It is hoped that they will thus help to maintain and further Eddington's concern for relating the scientific, the philosophical and the religious methods of seeking truth and will be a means of developing that insight into the unity underlying these different methods which was his characteristic aim.

Man's rapidly increasing control over natural forces holds out prospects of material achievements that are dazzling; but unless this increased control of material power can be matched by a great moral and spiritual advance, it threatens the catastrophic breakdown of human civilisation. Consequently, the need was never so urgent as now for a synthesis of the kind of understanding to be gained through various ways – scientific, philosophical and religious – of seeking truth. b b 4 9 3

In recent years it has become the custom of the Trustees to ask a distinguished scholar to deliver a short course of lectures which can then form the basis of a subsequent book. In the Michaelmas Term, 1980, this task was undertaken by Dr Charles Webster of the Wellcome Unit for the History of Medicine in the University of Oxford. It is a pleasure now to see his clear and learned account of the interpenetration of magic and mechanism from Paracelsus to Newton, to which we listened with such pleasure, being made available in a fuller form to a wider public by the publication of this monograph.

Trinity College, Cambridge
5 March 1982

J.C. Polkinghorne
Chairman of the Eddington Trustees

CONTENTS

TO JOSEPH NEEDHAM AND WALTER PAGEL

All things began in order, so shall they end, and so shall they begin again, according to the ordained order and mystical mathematicks of the city of heaven. *Garden of Cyrus*

PREFACE AND ACKNOWLEDGMENTS

The essays contained in this volume comprise a slightly modified version of the Eddington Lectures delivered in Cambridge in the autumn of 1980. The broad survey treatment of the original lectures has been maintained. Notwithstanding amplification of certain points in the published version, it is hoped that the spirit of the original lectures has been preserved. In the course of revision I have also tried where relevant to take account of literature published in the first half of 1981.

This short book is respectfully dedicated to Joseph Needham and Walter Pagel, both of whom have assisted the author in many different ways over the last fifteen years. These two scholars were drawn together by the events of the thirties, when, at Cambridge, they played an important part in pioneering the history of science. They became respectively chairman and secretary of the committee formed to promote the history of science in the University. Sir Arthur Eddington was one of the contributors to the volume of essays based on the first lecture series delivered under the auspices of this committee in 1936. The aims which Needham and Pagel expressed for the history of science in their introduction to this volume (*Background to Modern Science,* Cambridge, 1938), remain acceptable to many of us writing today. With respect to the present essays it is particularly noteworthy that Needham and Pagel have worked to broaden the base of the history of science by relating the process of discovery to the cultural environment in which science was prosecuted. They have also secured a new level of respect for the cultural values of renaissance natural philosophy, much of which was hitherto disregarded as irrelevant to the main currents of scientific thought. Among the benefits of their methods there emerged a much fuller appreciation of the religious motives of science. This latter theme is pertinent to the remit of the Eddington Lectures.

The author would like to express sincere thanks to the Eddington Trustees for their courteous hospitality, to Renate Burgess and William Schupbach for advice concerning illustrations, to Margaret Pelling for comments on the text and for editorial assistance, to Jean Loudon for invaluable typing assistance, and to Jonathan Barry for preparing the index. The author's many other debts to good friends will be evident from the notes to the text.

In quotations in the text standard contractions have been expanded, and in a few cases obvious errors have been silently corrected. Italicization in the originals has been omitted.

The Hartlib Papers at Sheffield University are cited with the kind permission of their owner Lord Delamere. The Evelyn Papers at Christ Church Oxford are cited by kind permission of The Trustees of the Will of Major Peter George Evelyn.

ILLUSTRATIONS

14. William Davisson, *Commentariorum in P. Severinus Ideam medicinae philosophicae* (The Hague, 1660), p.646. By courtesy of the Wellcome Trustees.

15. Title page from Comenius, *Didactica Opera Omnia*.

16. *Ars Moriendi* [Lyon, c.1490] after the Master ES. Reproduced by permission of the British Library Board.

17. *Ars Moriendi*, engraving by Carel de Mallerii after Jan van der Straet (d.1605). By courtesy of the Wellcome Trustees.

18. *Ars Moriendi*, engraving by Carel de Mallerii after Jan van der Straet (d.1605). By courtesy of the Wellcome Trustees.

19. Comenius, *Orbis pictus* (Nuremberg, 1658), emblem 149, 'Providentia dei'.

20. Frontispiece from Joseph Glanvill, *Saducismus Triumphatus* (London, 1681). By permission of the President and Fellows of Corpus Christi College, Oxford.

1 INTRODUCTION

One of the chief effects of the history of science as the subject has developed in the present century has been to drive a wedge between the cultures of Paracelsus and Newton. It may even seem like an act of perversity or lapsed historical judgement to bracket together the names of Paracelsus and Newton in the title of a book. By convention the two are regarded as inhabiting entirely discrete intellectual worlds. Our image of Newton is firmly associated with the values of the Enlightenment and the modern world, whereas the name of the enigmatic and inaccessible Paracelsus conveys alien associations of a tortured mind wrestling unsuccessfully to escape from the labyrinths of the dark ages.

Accounts of the 'Scientific Revolution' or 'Mechanization of the World Picture' have understandably concentrated on the appealing story of technical and conceptual innovation. As a natural adjunct to this operation, there is a tendency to generalize the distinctions between the dark age of pre-Copernicanism and the Enlightenment of Newtonianism. The remarkable extent of progress at the descriptive level in the sciences is thought to be correlated, and at least partly explained, by a similar transformation at the conceptual level. Often unwittingly, processes of selectivity have operated tending to highlight modern elements in the thought of Newton's generation, while discreetly allowing anything of a contrary nature to fall into the background. On the other hand, with respect to the generation of Paracelsus, there is a tendency to concentrate on credulity or vain respect for the authority of antiquity, while overlooking the wide evidence of critical analysis and independent judgement. By this means we have come to accept an almost perfect correlation between the rise of science and the decline of magic. Indeed the growth of the scientific movement is regarded as one of the primary manifestations of the demystification of the worldview occurring in the course of the seventeenth century. The above construction has its heroes and casualties. Newton is the premier hero, and Paracelsus is arguably the major casualty.

It is not the intention of the present essays to question the idea of the progress of science at the technical or descriptive level. According to separate, acceptable, and clearly defined criteria each of the natural sciences can be shown to have advanced, often in a spectacular manner, over the period between Paracelsus and Newton. It is also not my intention to suggest that there was nothing new in the new philosophies. But it is clear that there were remarkable elements of continuity sufficient to indicate an important degree of contiguity between the worldviews of the early sixteenth and late seventeenth centuries.

Paracelsus and Newton were not subsisting in intellectual worlds completely alien from one another. Both Paracelsus and Newton regarded assurance of personal salvation as their absolute priority. The working-out of the nature of humanity's relationship with the creator constituted their primary intellectual mission. Paracelsus contributed to the stream of reformation theology in which Newton was immersed. Among their contemporaries Neoplatonism was as much a vital force in the late seventeenth as in the early sixteenth century. Newton's acculturation occurred in the context of the ascendancy of the Cambridge Platonists. The situation at Cambridge represented a remarkable late echo of the Florentine Platonism of the renaissance, both schools being characterized by an intensity of fidelity to the spirit of ancient theology and philosophy.[1] The self-evident impact of Neoplatonism in England after 1660 should discourage any attempt to describe science at the time of the Royal Society in terms of the unquestioned dominance of the 'mechanical philosophy'.

The late revival of Neoplatonism in the seventeenth century and the eager absorption of this philosophy by the *avant garde* also brings into question the characterization of seventeenth century science in terms of the ascendancy of the 'moderns' over the 'ancients'. Paracelsus and the Neoplatonists were 'moderns' to the degree that they opposed the authority of scholasticism in theology and science, but 'ancients' in the manner of their adoption of a source of wisdom more venerable than scholasticism. The revolution towards which they worked was firmly rooted in the search for means of reviving the wisdom possessed by Moses, or Adam before the Fall.

Despite his celebrity as the conqueror of the ancients and founder of the propaganda platform of the new science, Francis Bacon also acknowledged a philosophical ancestry among the pre-Socratics and based his whole approach on the scriptural idea of return of man's dominion over nature, which was finally to counteract its sacrifice at the Fall. It is an interesting paradox that the very first manifesto in the ancients versus moderns controversy attacked the *modern* Galenic establishment and singled out Paracelsus as the reviver of *ancient* knowledge.[2]

This mode of representing modern science was purposely designed to appeal to the mentality of an age accustomed to the rhetoric of reformation theology, with its stress on the return of the church to the primitive purity of the early church fathers and more distant appeals to the model of the children of Israel. The famous defence of the moderns in *The History of the Royal Society* (1667), in openly drawing comparisons between the new science and the reformed church in England, represented nothing more than the application of a trusted tool which had been resharpened after long use by Francis Bacon and which was originally ground and honed to a fine edge by Paracelsus.

An important distorting element has been introduced into accounts of the rise of modern science through underestimation of the degree to which authors like Paracelsus, or authors belonging to the tradition of Neoplatonism or hermeticism, remained an integral part of the intellectual resources of the educated elite into the late seventeenth century. The magnitude of evidence indicative of the tenacity of interest in philosophies running contrary to the mechanical philosophy is so great that the only way of accommodating this vast anomaly has been to separate the leaders of science – judged representative men of their age – from the unrepresentative and more gullible majority. It is unfortunate for any proponent of this line that figures of outstanding importance, including Newton himself, turn out to display a lively interest in the occult. The only means of saving the phenomenon in this case is to adopt the unconvincing device of postulating a split personality for the scientists convicted of lapsing from consistent practice of the enlightenment ideal.

It is more realistic to come to terms with the persistence of the influence of figures such as Paracelsus, and to recognize that ideas falling into the non-mechanist tradition were not necessarily regarded by the scientists of later generations as the relics of an outmoded and scientifically unproductive dark age. Only recently have historians of science, largely upon stimulus from the outside, begun to appreciate the disadvantages to their craft of writing such figures as Paracelsus out of history.

It is particularly useful to take the example of Paracelsus because he is one of the principals from the pre-Copernican period thought to have least in common with the scientists of the late seventeenth century. We have been too prone to take at face value the image of Paracelsus as a deranged drunkard which derives almost entirely from a single, prejudiced pen, that of Johannes Oporinus.[3] The emotive violence directed against Paracelsus in the sixteenth century tends to be replaced in the modern literature by derision, even in the case of distinguished authorities as diverse as R. Lenoble and D.P. Walker.[4] It should be remembered that Oporinus's attempt to discredit Paracelsus on behalf of the humanists was totally unsuccessful at the time, and his letter should not be allowed to blind us to the virtually unimpeded rise of the influence of the medical reformer.

The degree to which Paracelsus stirred up the passions of his opponents is a measure of his success in sabotaging efforts aimed at permanently establishing the authority of Galen in the field of medicine. Thus the first major confrontation of the Scientific Revolution was between Paracelsus and Galen, rather than between Copernicus and Ptolemy. The significance of this confrontation was evident to contemporaries. In planning the first general history of medicine Le Clerc unhesitatingly placed Paracelsus at the beginning of the movement aimed at breaking completely with antiquity and constructing a completely new form of medicine from first principles. The respected sixteenth-century chronicler, Daniel Specklin, regarded the year 1517 as one of particular importance in the cultural history of Europe, marked by the efforts of Luther, Paracelsus and Dürer.[5] Paracelsus became known as the Luther of medicine, just as Kepler was to call himself the Luther of astrology. The comparison between Luther, Paracelsus and Dürer gains added weight from their combination of special interests and broader-ranging cultural concern.

Paracelsus was never regarded as a purely medical author. His speculations embraced every facet of the sciences and, like Newton, his biblical commentaries and religious works were both great in bulk and highly esteemed by their author, in comparison with his other writings. As far as Paracelsus was concerned, man and the cosmos were analogues which were inseparably linked. The study of man the microcosm was unthinkable without an appreciation of his place in the physical and spiritual macrocosm. What Paracelsus termed 'astronomy' always found a central place in his accounts of his medical system. This bias is reflected in the title of the major work of his maturity: *Astronomia Magna oder die Ganze Philosophia Sagus der Grossen und Kleinen Welt* (1537/8). Thus, although Paracelsus regarded his primary practical goal as the reform of medicine, his religious standpoint, repeated use of the microcosm-macrocosm analogy, and recognition of the powerful effects of the celestial environment on man, constantly threw him back into the fields of cosmology and cosmogony.

In asserting that the foundations of medicine lay in philosophy, astronomy and alchemy, Paracelsus was in line with an entrenched position established by medieval Arabic and Jewish medical authorities, and reflected in the prevailing bias of the medical education of his day. Natural philosophy and mathematics were taught as an appendage of medical education; astrology was a standard component of medical studies; alchemy occupied a small niche in the study of pharmacology. At the time of Paracelsus astrological treatises poured in abundance from the medical schools of Europe. Leading astronomers and cosmologers of the renaissance were educated as physicians; the two avocations were compatible and partly interchangeable. Rheticus was a successful physician. Copernicus studied medicine at Padua; Copernicus and Tycho Brahe cherished their skill as amateur medical practitioners. Even Kepler needed to resist pressure to devote himself primarily to the practice of medicine.

Paracelsus shared the traditional priorities, but his conception of philosophy, astronomy and alchemy was sharply different from that practised by the Arabs or in the schools, and he set out to refute most of what was customarily taught as the foundation for medical theory. His approach was thin on the technicalities of astronomy, but to a greater degree than his fellow astronomers he sketched out all aspects of the system, thus explaining the basis of interaction between the human, terrestrial, and celestial spheres. This desire for consistency and comprehensiveness persisted as a background concern for future generations of scientists. It remained important to Newton that his gravitational theory should be consistent with evidence concerning the workings of the terrestrial and human microcosm, and ideas from these latter areas were allowed to influence his thinking on metaphysical issues in general. It was unacceptable to Newton, as it had been to Paracelsus, to adopt physical principles at variance with evidence deriving from chemistry or physiology.

In view of the wide-ranging nature of his speculations it is not surprising that the influence of Paracelsus was felt well beyond the confines of medicine. His attraction to reformers was undiminishing. The influence of Paracelsus is evident in the cases of John Dee and Thomas Mouffet, two of the more adventurous and cosmopolitan English natural philosophers in the generation before Bacon.[6] Dee, even during the early, mathematical stage of his career, was collecting the works of Paracelsus with obsessive zeal. Mouffet interrupted his medical education at Cambridge to study among the Paracelsians at Basel, and declared Paracelsus to be the new Hippocrates. Mouffet managed to combine his aim of promoting Paracelsus with the more conventional task of completing Gesner's great *Historia Animalium*.

Gesner himself had regarded his fellow countryman Paracelsus with a mixture of admiration and fright, but the next generation, having access to the full body of posthumous works interlaced with beguiling spurious items, welcomed Paracelsus into the ranks of the philosophical reformers. The Paracelsians now became influential court physicians and philosophers. Three of this group, Petrus Severinus, Michael Sendivogius, and Oswald Croll, produced much-needed and accessible expositions of the ideas of Paracelsus, which greatly extended the philosophical life of their hero. Their primers remained actively consulted into the late seventeenth century. Severinus's *Idea medicinae philosophicae* (1571), Sendivogius's *Novum lumen chymicum* (1614), and Croll's *Basilica chymica* (1609) contained much of the rhetoric concerning the methodology and merits of experimental philosophy familiar to later generations through the writings of Francis Bacon. Croll's title page firmly established Paracelsus in the iconography of wisdom in science and medicine. Severinus was one of the few modern authors to wring an expression of sneaking regard from the author of the *Novum Organum*.[7]

Mouffet's defence of Paracelsus was addressed to Severinus and Tycho Brahe.[8] The latter was deeply interested in chemistry and medicine, and his indebtedness to the astronomy of Paracelsus will be mentioned below. Brahe attacked both Paracelsus's critic, Thomas Erastus, and Galenism, describing Paracelsus as 'Germanorum incomparabili Philosopho et Medico'.[9] Kepler was less directly interested in Paracelsus but he singled out Copernicanism and Paracelsianism as the most noteworthy features in the rise of modern knowledge.[10]

The ideas of Paracelsus were not rendered obsolete by the rise of the mechanical philosophy in the seventeenth century. Indeed evidence has mounted in a crucial area to suggest that the atomism of Gassendi owed much to a notorious circle of French chemists occupying an embattled position against the Galenist establishment in Paris.[11] The practical courses conducted by this group attracted a wide following, and they gave currency to theories of matter deriving from Paracelsus and the ancient atomists in various combinations. The atomism of Bacon can be shown to derive from a similar 'semi-Paracelsian' source.[12]

Paracelsianism was a phenomenon of the seventeenth as much as of the sixteenth century. French Paracelsianism was at its height between 1610 and 1650. English, Italian, and Scandinavian Paracelsianism are largely features of the period after 1650.[13] By this stage the partisans of Paracelsus were receiving new impetus owing to the wide diffusion and popularity of the works of Joan Baptista van Helmont. Robert Boyle was initiated into chemistry through predominantly Paracelsian and Helmontian sources. Notwithstanding Paracelsus's possible personal deficiencies Boyle accepted the justice of regarding him 'both in his own and after times [as] a very considerable person'.[14]

In Italy the merits of Paracelsus were urged by the physicians Pietro Castelli and Marc Aurelio Severino, in the case of the latter again in association with Democritean atomism and anatomy. In the next generation the Accademia degli Investiganti of Naples, one of the main centres for promoting the new philosophy in Italy, found no inconsistency in promoting the physics of Galileo and the medicine of Paracelsus and van Helmont. As in the case of their Parisian counterparts, the physicians who led the investigators found themselves locked in conflict with Galenists of the local College of Physicians. Their main manifesto bore

1. Title page of Oswald Croll, *Basilica chymica*.

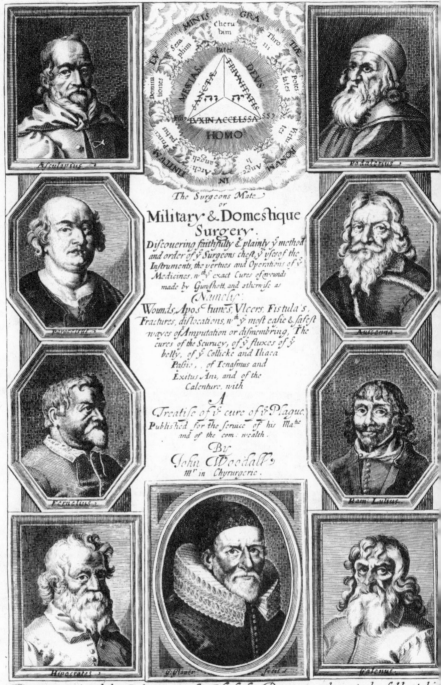

2.   Title page of John Woodall, *The Surgeons Mate*.

the characteristically Paracelsian title *Astronomiae microcosmicae systema novum*.[15]

In the later seventeenth century not only was Paracelsian chemical therapy practised on a wide scale by reputable practitioners, but the ideas of Paracelsus and van Helmont also exercised direct influence on theories of life and matter, as witness Glisson, Mayow, Willis, and others contributing to the golden age of English physiology.[16]

Paracelsus was by no means universally popular. Henry More viewed all Platonists having enthusiastic leanings with the deepest suspicion. Paracelsus he regarded as a dangerous adversary 'whose unbridled imagination and bold and confident obtrusion of his uncouth and supine inventions upon the world has . . . given occasion to the wildest Philosophical Enthusiasms that ever were broached by any either Christian or Heathen'. On the other hand, the retired enthusiast John Webster was unapologetic in citing Paracelsus as the primary source of inspiration of his solid and competent reviews, *Metallographia* (1671) and *The Displaying of Witchcraft* (1677). In his customary blunt way, Webster warned anyone who was offended by his 'too great Commendations to Paracelsus, Helmont, Basilius, and some other of the Adeptists, they may know that it is not without just cause, though they understand them not: for chewed meat must not always be put into men's mouths, let them study to find the depth of the meaning of those authors'.[17]

In view of the great influence in medical circles of his father's work it is not remarkable that Helmont's son, the exotic cabbalist Franciscus Mercurius van Helmont, was feted when he arrived in England in 1670, his ideas attracting the august attention of Lady Anne Conway, patroness of Henry More, and Lady Damaris Masham, the patroness of Locke and daughter of Ralph Cudworth. Franciscus Mercurius became an important contact between the Cambridge Platonists More and Cudworth and their allies in the low countries.[18]

Given these affiliations in the close vicinity of Newton, it is not surprising to find that Newton himself possessed a major edition of the works of Paracelsus, as well as the writings of Sendivogius, Croll, J.B. and F.M. van Helmont. These Paracelsian works represent a significant element in a notoriously large section of chemical and alchemical works in the Newton library.[19] The extent to which his copies of alchemical works were annotated, together with the great bulk of Newton's alchemical writings, gave rise to the celebrated epithet of Keynes that Newton was the last of the magicians.[20]

The final solution of the contentious issue of Newton's relations with alchemy remains tantalizingly beyond our reach for the moment. But the evidence of his library and papers indicates at the least that the literature of alchemy, hermeticism, and Paracelsian natural philosophy remained in vogue and was required reading among the serious scholars of Newton's generation. There persisted a strong sense of the possibility that embedded in the accretions of alchemical literature lay important truths expressed in symbolic form. To anyone immersed in decoding and unifying the symbolism of the Books of Daniel and Revelation, the hermetic literature would not offer insurmountable problems and the Paracelsians would seem entirely accessible. In view of the self-evident kinship between hermetic, alchemical, and scriptural sources, the deciphering of alchemical texts was an exercise that no scientific exegesist could resist. Newton and fellow adepts recognized no radical difference between their scientific and textual studies. The analogy between the book of nature and the book of revelation was a commonplace. To the scientist, commentary on alchemical texts represented the application of analytical skills to a vehicle of truth bearing kinship to both revelation and nature.

Continuing preoccupation in scientific circles with interpretation of the scriptures and related sources, and the obvious relevance of these exercises to the framing of the worldview of the scientists of the new age, cast serious doubt on the widely diffused idea that the separation of theology and science or the secularization of knowledge, latterly described in terms of the dissociation of sensibility, constituted dominant aspects of the scientific movement. Even Francis Bacon, father of the notion of the independence of experimental science, preserved a place for natural theology and exploited the scriptures and prophecies when determining the ethical standpoint of science. Arguably more representative were Alsted and Comenius who favoured the harmonization of knowledge from every major source. Their view was reflected by both Newton and Leibniz. The 'encyclopaedia' of Alsted or 'pansophia' of Comenius was based on the ideal of the perfect integration of truths devised by reason, or derived from experiment, scriptural sources, and ancient tradition. Perfect knowledge would be ratified by all sources, and the critical scientist of the seventeenth century accepted the challenge to effect this harmonization. Newton expressed the attraction of this idea when he recognized the 'admirable and new Paradox that Alchemy should have a concurrence with Antiquity and Theology', in an early commentary on an alchemical text.[21]

Somewhat inconveniently for standard interpretations of the Scientific Revolution the decades following the foundation of the Royal Society witness a last outburst of judicial astrology, the continuing flourishing of Paracelsian medicine, undiminishing appeal of alchemy and hermeticism, and the full fruition of Cambridge Platonism. Many traces of these movements are reflected among the activities of the membership of the Royal

Society, Newton perhaps providing the best example of all.[22]

From the historical point of view it is impossible to disregard the sources of evidence suggesting that non-mechanistic modes of scientific expression remained intellectually challenging to natural philosophers of all degrees of ability into the age supposedly dominated by the mechanical philosophy. It is therefore questionable whether the rise of science was associated with a total decline of magic as it was understood in Western society in the sixteenth and seventeenth centuries. No one doubts that at the village and popular level magic was to retain its traditional place well beyond the seventeenth century. Among the educated classes, there emerged a greater degree of scepticism concerning the cruder forms of manipulative magic, and judicial astrology along with its sister humoral pathology went out of favour at the end of the seventeenth century. But no later sceptics exceeded Paracelsus in the vehemence of their attack on judicial astrology or humoral pathology. The changes in fortune of judicial astrology should not attract attention away from the continuing appeal of such ideas as divine plenitude, metaphysical hierarchies, or the existence of fundamental harmonies and correspondences between the celestial and terrestrial world exercised through the intervention of a variety of spiritual agencies and intelligences. This animistic view of nature provided the intellectual underpinning for magic. At the least the magus might unlock the potential of occult qualities through exploiting natural magic; at the most he might gain spiritual ascendancy by transcending the limitations of the human frame. Magic as the performance of rituals aimed at controlling forces held responsible for the succession of events, slowly fell into abeyance among the intellectual elite, but it seems that the conceptual infrastructure of magic was maintained with conviction for a much longer period. Magic retained its appeal as a useful spiritual exercise, and it was also recognized as of value for medicine and relevant to scientific explanation. It is therefore important not to assume that the decline of popular operative magic entailed the wholesale abandonment of the magical worldview.

The following three chapters will explore three test cases relating respectively to prophecy, spiritual magic and demonic magic, to illustrate the difficulties involved in exaggerating the extent of the epistemological shift occurring between the ages of Paracelsus and Newton. It may then cease to surprise that Manuel's epitome of Newton could be applied almost verbatim to Paracelsus: 'The more Newton's theological and alchemical, chronological and mythological work is examined as a whole corpus, set by the side of his science, the more apparent it becomes that in his moments of grandeur he saw himself as the last of the interpreters of God's will in actions, living on the eve of the fulfilment of times'.[23]

For the purpose of this comparison it is appropriate to concentrate to some extent on evidence deriving from Germany at the time of the Reformation and England during the Restoration. The approach adopted in the present essays is now no longer unfamiliar. As is evident from the footnotes, a mounting body of comment shares a similar point of view. It is hoped that exercises of this kind will contribute towards a more balanced historical perspective on the body of speculations about nature produced in the sixteenth and seventeenth centuries. We need to reconsider some deeply held opinions concerning the general cultural relevance of the new science. In particular there is a risk that science is bearing too much of the explanatory burden with respect to the important issue of the decline of the magical worldview. The dominance of the mechanical philosophy is exaggerated and this construct is handled too simplistically. It seems possible that the new science was accompanied by a less radical epistemological shift than has hitherto been thought likely.

Over-reliance on old categories has led to questionable results. The 'mechanical philosophy' tends to be regarded as a water-tight compartment the characterization of which is determined by reference to a handful of classic works by figures of the stature of Descartes or Boyle. It is tempting to adopt 'hermeticism' as the alternative category, and to dragoon the efficient personnel of science into the former and the inefficient into the latter. This proceeding conforms to deep prejudices imposed by modern scientific ideology. In reality the worldview of the Scientific Revolution should be viewed as a diverse phenomenon, the result of a dynamic interplay of forces which emanated from many different directions. All of these forces contributed to the process of creativity and change, and none of them deserves to be written off *a priori* as a useless intellectual encumbrance from a discredited magical past.

NOTES

1. E. Cassirer, *The Platonic Renaissance in England* (London, 1953) – still the best review. For more recent literature see, C.A. Staudenbaur (1974), Platonism, Theosophy, and Immaterialism: Recent Views of the Cambridge Platonists, *Journal of the History of Ideas*, **35**, 157–69.

2. R.F. Jones, *Ancients and Moderns*, 2nd edn (Berkeley and Los Angeles, 1965).

3. W. Pagel, *Paracelsus* (Basel, 1958), pp.29–31. By contrast with Oporinus, the respected astronomer Rheticus met Paracelsus and formed a totally favourable opinion of him, W. Hubicki, Paracelsists in Poland, in A.G. Debus, ed., *Science, Medicine and Society in the Renaissance. Essays to honor Walter Pagel*, 2 vols (New York, 1972), **1**, 167–8.

4. R. Lenoble, *Mersenne ou la Naissance du Mécanisme*, 2nd edn (Paris, 1971), pp.136–7, attributes to Paracelsus the characters of Dr Faust and Dr Knock, while D.P. Walker, *Spiritual and Demonic Magic from Ficino to Campanella* (London, 1958), p.103, prefers James Thurber.

5. Daniel Le Clerc, *Histoire de la Médecine*, 2nd edn (Amsterdam, 1723), p.792; Daniel Specklin, *Les Collectanées*, ed. R. Reuss (Strasbourg, 1890), p.487.

6. C. Webster, Alchemical and Paracelsian medicine, in Webster ed., *Health, Medicine and Mortality in the Sixteenth Century* (Cambridge, 1979), pp.301–34.

7. B. Farrington, ed., *The Philosophy of Francis Bacon* (Liverpool, 1964), pp.18, 57,66,71. For Croll's title page see illustration 1 (p.7) and for one of many echoes, illustration 2 (p.8) from the famous surgical work of Woodall.

8. Mouffet, *De jure et praestantia chymicorum medicamentorum* (Frankfurt, 1584).

9. Brahe to Brucaeus, 1589, *Opera Omnia*, ed. J.L.E. Dreyer, 15 vols (Copenhagen, 1913–1929), **7**, 169–75.

10. Kepler, *De stella nova* (1606), *Gesammelte Werke*, ed. W. von Dyck, M. Caspar *et al.*, 19 vols (Munich, 1937–), **1**, 331–2.

11. H. Metzger, *Les doctrines chimiques en France du début du XVIIe à la fin du XVIIIe siècle* (Paris, 1923); O.R. Bloch, *La Philosophie de Gassendi* (The Hague, 1971), pp.236–74 and *passim*.

12. J.R. Partington, *A History of Chemistry*, vol.3 (London, 1962), pp.1–8. G. Rees (1975), Francis Bacon's Semi-Paracelsian Cosmology, *Ambix*, **22**, 81–101.

13. C. Webster, *The Great Instauration: Science, Medicine and Reform, 1626–1660* (London, 1975), pp.273–82; S. Lindroth, *Paracelsismen i Sverige till 1600 – talets mitt* (Uppsala, 1943).

14. Robert Boyle, *Works*, ed. T. Birch, 6 vols (London, 1772), **2**, 262; see also p.101.

15. M.H. Fisch, The Academy of the Investigators, in E.A. Underwood, ed., *Science, Medicine and History. Essays in Honour of Charles Singer*, 2 vols (London, 1953), **1**, 521–63; N. Badaloni, *Introduzione a G.B. Vico* (Milan, 1961), pp.25–37 and *passim;* M. Torrini, *Tommaso Cornelio e la Ricostruzione della Scienza* (Naples, 1977).

16. Slightly less appreciative than Pagel of the Paracelsian contribution is R.G. Frank Jr, *Harvey and the Oxford Physiologists: A Study of Scientific Ideas* (Berkeley and Los Angeles, 1980).

17. Henry More, *Enthusiasmus Triumphatus* (1656), Section XLV, ix, quoted from *A Collection of Several Philosophical Writings* (London, 1662), p.36; John Webster, *Metallographia* (London, 1671), sig.B2v.

18. A. Coudert Gottesman, F.M. van Helmont: His Life and Thought, unpublished Ph.D. dissertation, University of London 1972; *idem* (1976), A Quaker–Kabbalist Controversy, *Journal of the Warburg and Courtauld Institutes,* **39**, 171–89.

19. J. Harrison, *The Library of Isaac Newton* (Cambridge, 1978).

20. J.M. Keynes, in Royal Society, *Newton Tercentenary Celebrations* (Cambridge, 1947), pp.27–34.

21. Newton, Manna, Cambridge University Library Microfilm, Keynes MS 33, f.5r.

22. K.T. Hoppen (1976), The Nature of the Early Royal Society, *British Journal for the History of Science*, **9**, 1–24, 243–73.

23. F.E. Manuel, *The Religion of Isaac Newton* (Oxford, 1974), p.23.

2   PROPHECY

Accounts of the Scientific Revolution are understandably dominated by astronomy and cosmology. *De revolutionibus orbium coelestium* by Copernicus was published in 1543, two years after the death of Paracelsus. Coincidentally Vesalius's *De humani corporis fabrica* was also published in 1543. These two works are thought to have set the seal on the demise of Paracelsus's reputation in two of the main spheres in which he operated. The year 1543 accordingly seems to mark an important stage in disentangling astronomy from the sciences of man. The latter progressively abandoned obscure astronomical analogies as their basis, in favour of the findings of gross anatomy and experimental physiology. Copernicanism did not directly confront judicial astrology, but there can be no doubt that the Copernicans of the seventeenth century led the trend against judicial astrology, so finally emancipating astronomy from its bondage under medicine.

The Copernican Revolution provides the blueprint for the Scientific Revolution as a whole. As in the course of the seventeenth century the Copernican model was supplied with a firm foundation in the field of celestial mechanics, so at the metaphysical level the idea was gradually established that the celestial system was a stable entity operating according to the same laws as were evident in the terrestrial field. Though God played some positive role in this process His presence was pushed far back in time to the creation of the heavenly clockwork. It is assumed that the mechanical philosopher came to regard God as a remote law-giver. The religious goals of science were formally preserved by identifying exhaustive investigation into the laws of nature as a kind of religious exercise, by means of which the scientist might be translated into a Christian Virtuoso. Notwithstanding the obvious risks of Deism, the religious value of this exercise was still being maintained up to the eve of the publication of *The Origin of Species*.

Nevertheless, Copernicanism also developed against a background of Christian belief which regarded the earth as a creation limited in its duration to a few thousand years. By analogy with the creation story the history of the world was generally condensed into six periods, each of a thousand years, with the seventh being regarded as the eschatological era. The ages of the earth and the stages of civilization were thought to be ascertainable on the basis of biblical chronology. Christian civilization was not seen as a phenomenon destined for permanency. Most estimates placed the Reformation after the fifth millennium in the pre-ordained sequence. Having undergone trials of various kinds, the Christian West was, according to most accounts, being prepared for an imminent Day of Judgment, in association, it was hoped, with an *Annus Magnus, Annus Platonicus*, or Golden Age for the elect.

This acute sense of imminent reward and punishment was to remain a persistent feature of Western European thought in the sixteenth and seventeenth centuries, and it set an important limitation on any vision of the cosmos as some kind of perpetual motion. John Webster represented a strong tradition when insisting that there was 'not in God a rude, passive permission, separate from the positive and active decree, order and will of his Divine Providence and Government, but that he doth rule all things according to the power and determination of his own positive and actual will'.[1] The idea of God as a monarch, not content with *ordinary* providence, but exercising *extraordinary* powers over the destiny of His creation, wielding this monarchy to determine eventualities proportionately to the deserts of every section of the human race, could not have been regarded as an irrelevance to science, or as a passing curiosity.

Knowledge enhanced the sense of trial and impermanence. God's retribution seemed more imminent to the contemporaries of Paracelsus or Newton, than the possibility of a nuclear holocaust seems to us. Accordingly questions relating to the more permanent features of world systems or planetary mechanisms arguably took second place, among the educated public, to cosmological considerations bearing on the immediate future of Christian Europe. Experts were accordingly faced with the delicate problem of bringing their cosmology into line with eschatology. Moreover their particular technical skills were recognized as potentially useful for evaluating the sources of evidence relating to eschatology. They were therefore in a position to offer informed speculation on the sensitive issue of the precise place of their age in the preordained pattern of events forming the climax of universal history. This complex analytical exercise posed a major challenge to the scientific intellect of the modern age. The debate entered into at the time of Paracelsus had lost none of its fascination by the date of publication of Newton's *Principia*.

In the early Christian period prophecy was an important ingredient in the framework of magical knowledge. The ability to understand the purposeful connection of events according to their succession in time, and to issue predictions which were fulfilled, was offered as a sign of genuine inspiration, and a test for distinguishing between true and false revelation. The Christian church was never entirely successful in limiting the authority of revelation to the documents of the Old and New Testaments, or in imposing its own views of the interpretation of the prophetic books of these scriptures. The middle ages produced its own rash of prophecies, among which the idea of an imminent millennium was given currency by the Joachimites. With the advent of printing the accumulated ancient and medieval sources of prophecy became an object of widespread interest. The emphasis now gradually switched from framing new predictions to deciphering the multitude of biblical and non-biblical prophecies.

Prophecy was regarded by Paracelsus as the highest form of magic.[2] He outlined three types of prophecy: the first, astronomy, provided clues concerning the course of history by its direct reference to the heavens in which the plan of history was drawn out for our benefit. Secondly, magical images and oracles were infused with the virtues of the stars and these were subject to interpretation in the same way that the doctor charted the course of a disease. Finally, the prophecies of Christ himself were incorporated into the scriptures. Reference to all three realms of knowledge was necessary in order to establish the shorter and longer term prospects for Christian Europe.

For Paracelsus and his contemporaries prophecy assumed a direct importance. Europe was self-evidently in the grip of a major crisis which was striking at the foundations of secular and religious order. Paracelsus witnessed this turmoil in centres like Strasbourg, Basel, Salzburg, and St Gallen in the course of his wanderings, and the turbulence of his own career was a reflection of the instability of the times. Each faction regarded itself as the agent of purification and looked for the resolution of the crisis in its own favour in the interval before the Day of Judgment. In the apocalyptic atmosphere of the Reformation and Radical Reformation there was no sense that creation was a stable entity destined to run its course for an unlimited duration. The instability of history was translated into cosmological terms. It was a major utility of astrology that while fully admitting the gravity of degenerative trends, its cyclical apparatus admitted the hope of future amelioration. With varying degrees of sophistication celestial events were interpreted to reinforce the political message. Astrology thus assumed a significant political purpose. Luther's scepticism and overt antagonism towards astrology were not widely shared: his henchman Melanchthon demonstrated unwavering faith in the significance of astrological signs. It was widely believed that Charles V was driven to abdicate and live the life of a recluse playing with mechanical toys, because of forebodings concerning the spectacular comet of 1586 expressed by his physician and mathematician Paul Fabricius. Other examples could be given of princes seeking guidance or justification from astrological sources.

A major display of the talents of orthodox astrology had been witnessed by Paracelsus at an early stage in his career, with the arrival of the conjunction of all the planets in the sign of Pisces during February 1524. Between 1517 and 1524, according to one estimate, no fewer than 133 tracts composed by fifty-six different authors were devoted to the 1524 conjunction.[3] Almost to a man learned astronomers regarded this event with alarm: a flood of catastrophic proportions was the obvious major portent, but in the event of this being spared, Europe would experience severe weather, bad harvests, social unrest, a revolt of the peasants, and attempts to overthrow the established religious and secular order. In the event, the combination of relatively normal climate and stirrings of the Peasants' Revolt provided comfort for both astrologers and their critics, everyone finding something to justify their prognostications.

As the literature surrounding the 1524 conjunction demonstrates, astrology was by no means a unified, uncritical or unchanging art. Cornelius Agrippa von Nettesheim did much to popularize the ideas of Ficino on astrology and the harmony between the macrocosm and microcosm, but he was highly critical of judicial astrology as it was customarily practised, and he attacked naive faith in horoscopes.[4] Yet he himself made predictions and believed in principle that high value could be attached to predictions based on the correlation of evidence of portents and signs, terrestrial and celestial, taken together with critical analysis of evidence from scriptural and other inspired sources. Agrippa was drawn to publish at least one specific prognostication, probably in the context of the 1524 conjunction, for which he adopted the dominant pessimistic forecast for immediate events, but at the end offered the hope that in the future peace would reign throughout the earth.[5]

A less sophisticated attempt to reform astrology emanated from Johannes Indagine (von Hagen), a priest of Steinheim, near Frankfurt, who was, with better reason than Agrippa, suspected of favouring the Reformation. Indagine's own work owed its popularity to linking a reformed 'natural astrology' with elementary discussions of chiromancy and physiognomy.[6] Association with Indagine, emphasized in a letter printed in the *Introductiones apotelesmaticae,* seems to lie at the root of the scientific interests of Otto Brunfels, another recent convert to the protestant position.[7] Brunfels's famous *Herbarum vivae icones* (1531) is recognized as a landmark in the history of botany, similar in major respects, although not quite as significant as *De humani corporis fabrica* of Vesalius. Brunfels applied his energies in many directions, his greatest mark upon contemporaries arising from his notoriety as the first explicit defender of Nicodemism, which earned him the scorn of Calvin. Brunfels established a distinct position with respect to astrology, closely allied to the theme running throughout his writings that despite the corruption of the church and the wickedness of rulers, the oppressed were not justified in open revolt: the punishment of tyrants was the office of God rather than of men. The tables were turned on the radicals by firmly identifying as Antichrist, not the corrupt regime of the papacy, but rather those seeking to overthrow established authority.[8]

This point of view was expressed in his *Almanac and Prognostication from 1526 to the end of this and all worlds*, a tract intentionally bearing a superficial resemblance to ostentatious prognostications then in circulation; on closer inspection it emerges as a thinly disguised parody designed to subvert traditional astrology, and marshal biblical texts to reinforce a quietist acceptance of the workings of providence.[9] Having demolished one major dimension of astrology, Brunfels immediately retrenched, in deference to his long-held view that astrology was essential to the art of medicine. He went on to issue two minor writings on medical astrology, going against the Arabist bias of his teacher Indagine to attack the tradition of astrology identified with Avicenna. Paradoxically Brunfels's final words on astrology were published as an appendix to a work by his associate Nicolaus Prückner, an active contributor to the literature of prognostication, whose own contribution contained a lively defence of astrology against the criticisms of theologians. Consequently although Brunfels became one of the most widely read and republished of the more popular astrological writers, the message of his *Almanac* was ultimately obscured.

Among contemporaries the Brunfels *Almanac* and a few other writings of a similar disposition provided much-needed propaganda for authorities who were coming to realize in the light of the recent Peasants' Revolt that fears and predictions of civil unrest might become self-fulfilling. Prophecies in circulation gave grounds for these fears. The famous frontispiece to Reynmann's *Practica* of 1524, graphically indicated the confrontation between the peasantry and the ecclesiastical establishment under the sign of Pisces. More directly threatening were the activities of an itinerant preacher and medical practitioner like Melchior Hofmann, whose sectarian programme was in 1526 heightened by his exposition of Daniel predicting the end of the world in 1533.[10] He was soon to arrive on Brunfels's home territory of Strasbourg, where he was declared to be the new Elijah. His new home was expected to become the scene for the final apocalyptic conflict and establishment of the new Jerusalem.

In view of the contradictions and complications in the astrological debate, it is not surprising that the position of Paracelsus is not easy to define. He was, as much as Ficino or Agrippa, committed to a metaphysic conducive to astrology, yet like Brunfels he attacked the simplistic formulae and uncritical assertions which dominated popular astrology.

Practica vber die grossen vnd ma-
nigfeltigen Coniunction der Planeten/die im
jar M. D. XXiiij. erscheinen/vñ vnge-
zweiffelt vil wunderparlicher
ding geperen werden.

Leonhart Rynman.

Auß Rŏ.Kay.May.Gnaden vnd Freihaiten/hüt sich menigklich/diese meine Practica in zwayen jaren nach zütrucken bey verlierung. 4.Marck lŏtige Golts.

3.   Title page of Leonhart Reynmann, *Practica uber . . . Coniunction der
Planeten*.

As indicated above he was in no doubt that astronomy was fundamental to the art of medicine, and integrally relevant to the art of prophecy. These two functions were inseparable. For true understanding it was necessary to pay attention to all the workings of heaven – to be a theologian, philosopher and physician. To attempt to isolate the medical aspect of astrology was to offend against God.[11] Paracelsus was thus opposed to the attempt of those like Brunfels to circumscribe the operation of astrology, and, while he was in favour of a non-sectarian unity of believers, he was as vigorously opposed as Calvin to the dissembling of the Nicodemites.

For Paracelsus it was essential to monitor all cosmic events both with respect to their normal regularized workings, and also because special cosmic signs were related to special interventions by God in the history of mankind. The proof for such correlations lay in such wonders as the star warning of the birth of Christ in Bethlehem, and in other events recorded in the bible. At these times God had left to one side the normal workings of the 'outer Heavens', in order to interfere with the more potent forces of the 'inner Heavens'. In the biblical age God had worked to punish the wicked and reward the virtuous; in the later ages God's hand was at work in wars, pestilence, and famine, all of which might be seen as His punishment, and a step towards the renovation of the world.

Paracelsus warned that these operations, put into effect frequently and of many different kinds, were not done without reason, but were aimed by God as a punishment of our vices. These signs in the heavens were God's writings there, corresponding with the words of Christ spoken on earth, both being granted us to secure repentance. Only the most meticulous attention to changes within the celestial and terrestrial environment would enable us to ascertain whether phenomena represented the ordinary course of natural events, or an extraordinary occurrence warning us of some cataclysm in the near future.[12] It was clear to Paracelsus that the world was not eternal, and that the Day of Judgment was fast approaching. The days were running out; soon a new paradise, or new Hebron would be established; ultimately the elect would be reborn in a new creation.[13]

Recurrent reference to the above eschatological sequence is detectable throughout the scientific, medical and theological writings of Paracelsus. For instance in the biological context it was suggested that God had predetermined the pool of hereditary factors so that ultimately the range of recombinations of characteristics would be exhausted. This point would mark the onset of the Day of Judgment: 'At that moment the hour has run out for the first world'.[14] The different ages and monarchies of the world would be over. The monarchies of Israel and Christianity would then give way to the monarchy of the spirit. Men may appear to have achieved final rule, but Christ would soon come and drive these merchants out of the temple. The rule of the false Christs could not extend beyond the precise periods stated in Daniel and Revelation.[15]

The first major prophetic exercise of Paracelsus was his commentary on the much discussed *Prognostication* (*Pronosticatio in latino*, 1488) by Johannes Lichtenberger, an eclectic compilation which gave added currency to Joachimite prophecy by incorporating elements from Arabic astrology.[16] Indagine regarded Lichtenberger as a model for his own 'natural astrology'. No doubt Indagine was also attracted by the potentialities of Lichtenberger's work as political propaganda. This opportunity was eagerly seized while interest in the *Prognostication* was at its most intense following the Peasants' Revolt, when the text was issued thirteen times in five years.[17] Luther himself was driven to issue an edition, his introductory remarks aiming partly to forestall the use of the prophecies by the Catholic faction, partly to transfer the identity of the devil with horns from himself to Thomas Müntzer, an attribution which Paracelsus promptly returned to Luther.[18] The commentary on Lichtenberger by Paracelsus is outstanding for its length, originality and perceptiveness.[19] Somewhat surprisingly Paracelsus emerges as entirely unsympathetic to the Lichtenberger approach to prophecy, and proves to be quite as much a sceptic as Luther himself concerning attempts to plot the immediate course of European history by combining evidence from astrology and oracles.

With shrewd insight into the psychology of the prophet, Paracelsus argued that Lichtenberger's view of the future was determined by his French patrons and paymasters, with the result that the future salvation of Christian Europe seemed to rest on the likelihood of French domination. Furthermore Lichtenberger was committing the inveterate error of unreformed astrology in attributing divine purpose to events which represented the normal course of the cosmic order, and consequently falling into a form of astrological determinism which failed to take account of the fundamental gift of free will. The great impact of the normal cycle of cosmic events, and of perturbations in these events should not be taken as an automatic sign of punishment from God, and of the inability of man to control his diseases or destiny. Such resignation to adverse forces, some of which genuinely emanate from the stars, is to underestimate the power of man to compensate for adversity. God had granted man by special favour an inner capacity to resist the outer influences of the stars. Exercise of his spiritual capacity permits man to rise above the heavens to the level of God. Thereby man might rule over the stars, and crush their influence as a worm is trodden underfoot.

Thus, in the course of the year, it snows, or rains, hails, and is hot or cold; this is how the heavens constitute the year, and it should be understood that the heavens work in us in a similar way. But we are much stronger than the year, for we can ward off the weather, and seek out the good at the expense of the bad. For we have in ourselves an everlasting summer, which is never without fruit or flowers. And that is the summer which will come when no more years will be numbered, but all years will seem like the briefest moment. Thus we should mobilize our inner powers, so that we are not directed by the heavens but by our wisdom. For if we forget this wisdom, so are we like beasts and shall live as reeds in the water and not know from one moment to the next from whence a gust will come and where we will be blown.[20]

It was in this frame of mind that the elect should face the future, wary of the powers of the stars to corrupt, but determined to overcome the forces of evil. The future general course of events was clear from biblical sources; the fine details elaborated by astrologers were unimportant. The conflict between the true and the false Christian church was reaching its climax. Somewhat unconventionally Paracelsus insisted that the prophecies pointed to the overthrow of all opponents of Christ, rather than relating specifically to the Turks. Uprisings by peasants marked the beginning of the climactic struggle against the 'Turks'; the peasantry was alerted not to sacrifice its primitive virtue; the next eight years would be marked by warfare and there would be great bloodshed in 1535. After that the revolution of the heavens would be completed, and the circle of the world would come under the rule of Christ himself.

Almost as enticing to the student of prophecy as the Lichtenberger prophecies were the Nuremberg figures, a Joachimite source considerably changed in the course of its journey into the hands of sixteenth-century commentators. A commentary on the Nuremberg figures provided the occasion for the first venture into astrology and prophecy by Andreas Osiander, an aspiring local Lutheran minister who was to attain a reflected glory as author of the introductory letter to *De revolutionibus orbium coelestium* (1543) by Copernicus – this letter being subject to almost as many interpretations by historians of astronomy as the Nuremberg figures themselves.[21] Confronted by a line of emblems illustrating the troubles of the popes, followed by a sequence of angelic popes, Osiander earned the applause of protestantism by sliding out Celestine V, and inserting Martin Luther in Celestine's place at the beginning of the angelic line. Osiander was to become best known for *Conjectures on the End of the World*, which appeared in its Latin edition in 1544, quickly followed by German (1545) and English (1548). This work was important in directing attention to the possibilities of combining prophecy and chronology.

Paracelsus gave no support to the crude propaganda of Osiander, as ever firmly resisting pressure for sectarian alignment. But he fully accepted that magic figures were a potential source of truth concerning human destiny, as valid as the evidence of astrology. His commentary kept firmly to moral questions and concentrated on elaborating the various ways in which the papacy had transgressed and become absorbed in worldly values. In the Lichtenberger commentary he had denied that the Holy Roman Empire would ever be dissolved; now he was satisfied that the Nuremberg figures provided significant proof that the papal power would be irrevocably destroyed.[22]

Paracelsus must have been dissatisfied with the relatively unspecific conclusions of his interpretation of the Nuremberg figures. In the absence of suitable antique sources he resorted to commenting on a set of thirty-two figures of his own devising paralleling the thirty in the Nuremberg sequence, but quite different and more diverse in character, looking forward to the emblem books which were to become a great fashion later in the century. The *Prophecy for the next twenty four years* (1536) encapsulated his views on the immediate prospects for Christian Europe. He agreed with other commentators that the signs were pointing to a period of turbulence; the 'time for the people' had arrived and the mutation of the world would be accomplished, ending in the unification of the elect with the godhead, and the final dissolution of the present monarchy.[23]

The emblems themselves were intelligently constructed. For the most part the text reinforced the message of his commentary on the Nuremberg figures, while more direct political comment was contained in supplementary prophecies. The general line of argument was clear; the wicked may seem to prosper yet their punishment was inevitable. Only in the last few figures did Paracelsus pass from elaborating the fate of the damned, to illuminating the hopes for the elect. This change would be preceded by a major eclipse of the sun, followed by great floods, uprisings, and war which would spread throughout the northern lands. Then the French kingdom would decline, and the rich be disinherited and struck down by the Turks. After this the better times would come. It was predicted that by 1542 the elect would be unified, and that by 1555 the light would have come, preparing for the final fulfilment of the prophecies. Although 1560 was marked for this last event, Paracelsus expressed himself cautiously when considering whether the whole sequence would be accomplished within the span of a human lifetime. But his inclusion of specific dates indicates commitment to an early date for the onset of the final assault on Antichrist. The last days on earth were depicted emblematically as scenes of childlike innocence and joy, and as a state of permanent rest (see illustration 10, p. 50). The ultimate golden age was described with all the

]ßlegung des Com=
meten erſchynen im hochbirg/ zů
mitlem Augſten/ Anno 1 5 3 1. Durch
den hochgelertenn Herren
Paracelſum.zc.

17

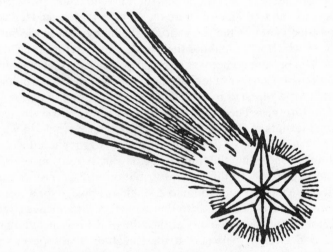

4.   Title page of Paracelsus, *Usslegung des Commeten . . . Anno 1531.*

characteristic imagery of the scriptures and classical sources.

The more general prophetic writings of Paracelsus were interspersed among shorter tracts making predictions for shorter spans, or occasioned by particular events. Perhaps the most important was his account of the comet which appeared to the north-west of St Gallen on 12 August 1531, shortly after Paracelsus's arrival in the town.[24] This was Paracelsus's introduction to Halley's comet, and it was as if this meeting was providentially arranged. The comet had made its appearance at a sensitive moment and was observed from a sensitive location: the area had experienced bad harvests in 1529 and 1530; the economic plight of the population was worsened by disruption of trade owing to political conflicts; the Swiss confederation was rapidly sliding into war; St Gallen was experiencing the height of the conflict between Anabaptists, Zwinglians and Catholics. Paracelsus opened his review on the grave note that 'Each destruction of a monarchy, and when each one is raised at God's behest, is announced by indications and signs, so that everyone will be able to recognize the destruction or ruin, and have forewarning of such monarchies and their fall or rise'. Comets in particular, being abnormal creations of sporadic occurrence, were regarded as particularly portentous. The seriousness of such an event was confirmed when its appearance coincided with independent evidence drawn from the scriptures, histories and oracles. In this case Paracelsus announced that the appearance of the comet might have been predicted from the outbreaks of epidemics which had been witnessed in the vicinity.

This commentary on the comet of 1531 summed up much of what Paracelsus had written elsewhere on astronomy. His readers were asked to consider what was the relevance of the many signs in the heavens and on earth which were making their appearance during the current hard times. The present comet was to be taken as a sure sign of an impending disruption of the order of monarchies. The tone was overwhelmingly pessimistic; little was said to prompt expectation of an imminent improvement in fortunes. There was scant comfort in such a document for the spiritual leaders of Zürich, Leo Jud and Ulrich Zwingli, to whom it was sent by Paracelsus. No doubt the prophecy was regarded as confirming local fears concerning the imminence of war. Arrangements were made for the immediate printing and distribution of Paracelsus's tract, but it was too late for it to contribute to Zwingli's campaign for a better state of war preparedness. Zürich drifted into conflict with the five states and on 10 October Zwingli and many of the elite of Zürich, including the father of Conrad Gesner, perished at the slaughter of Kappel, so putting a peremptory end to the intellectual and spiritual leadership of Zwinglian reform. There could be no more potent reminder of the power of prognostication.[25]

Even the more sympathetic modern commentators on Paracelsus tend to pass over his prophetic writings without more than incidental comment. These works are regarded as little more than a penumbra to the writings more directly relevant to medical reform. However this does not reflect Paracelsus's own estimate of their importance, nor that of his contemporaries. Paracelsus was largely known to his public through the prophetic and astronomical tracts, which were the only class of his writings to be published without delay. Indeed, with one major and a couple of minor exceptions, they were the only works of Paracelsus published during his lifetime, and they were frequently reissued in German and Latin forms. An accessible collected edition, *Astronomica et Astrologica*, edited by Balthazar Flöter, appeared in 1567. Prophecies by Paracelsus became a standard part of widely distributed anthologies of such writings. The commentary on the Nuremberg figures seems to have been the first of the writings of Paracelsus to be translated into English.[26] Echoes of the 'prophecies' of Paracelsus are found in the works of William Lilly and others in the mid-seventeenth century, and finally Paracelsus joins Lichtenberger and Nostradamus in earning the dubious distinction of being found relevant to every major period of crisis up to the present day.

Comets occupied a central place in the cosmology and astronomical writings of Paracelsus. He was contributing to a debate which attracted the widest interest. The character of the popular fascination with comets was graphically expressed by Grant: 'every feature in their appearance was gazed upon with intense anxiety, and was assimilated, by the influence of an excited imagination, to the awe-inspiring lineament of a supernatural phantom'.[27] It is not surprising that the comet features prominently in Dürer's *Melencolia I*.[28] It is important to consider whether comets became deprived of their magical significance as they became better observed by the astronomers of the new age.

Recent researches have greatly extended our insight into the scope and role of astrology in the sixteenth and seventeenth centuries. The persistence of astrology at the popular level comes as no surprise. But it is also clear that among the educated public and even within expert circles the debate about the relationship between the cosmic and the terrestrial order remained very much alive throughout the seventeenth century. The basic lines of argument would have been quite familiar to Paracelsus or Agrippa. But at the same time the physical sciences advanced and astronomy changed and matured beyond recognition. Among the scientific intellectuals judicial astrology became relegated to the position of an amusing but worthless diversion. No doubt Agrippa would not have gone this far, but Paracelsus would have concurred entirely. It remains to be considered how much of the basic framework adopted by Paracelsus on the issues discussed above was found unacceptable in the later period. Were the generations experiencing the mechanization of the worldview, driven towards a fundamental change of attitude with respect to the close causal inter-relationship between celestial and terrestrial, on the question of divine superintendence over the course of human history, on the relevance of signs, or, finally, on the unity of scientific, prophetic, and scriptural explanation?

5.   Albrecht Dürer, 'Melencolia I' – copy.

The arrival of Copernican astronomy in itself seems not to have occasioned a fundamental shift of opinion on the above questions. A good example of the link between Paracelsus and the founders of modern astronomy is provided by reference to the early astronomical writings of Tycho Brahe, relating to the new star of 1572 and the comet of 1577. The acknowledged expert in the history of this field recognizes the popularity of the comet tracts by Paracelsus, but compares him unfavourably with other observers of the comets of the 1530s, especially Peter Apian. We are warned that Paracelsus 'must have been a deterrent to progress in this field', the result being a time lag before Tycho Brahe produced observations according to an entirely new standard of accuracy.[29]

Closer inspection demonstrates that Tycho Brahe was by no means alienated by the speculations of the earlier period. His tract containing an account of the new star of 1572 briefly concluded that this remarkable event presaged disturbances in the north of Europe which would spread elsewhere and prepare the way for a new secular and religious order.[30] The appearance of what seemed to be the first new star since the star of Bethlehem gave considerable grounds for reflection. Among the more ingenious observations, it was pointed out that the nova had blazed for seventeen lunar months and then vanished twice seven years before the first lunar eclipse predicted for the fateful year of 1588 (as well as 171 lunar months 111 days before the second eclipse), when Saturn, Jupiter and Mars would meet in the moon's house. Such observations could be tied up with a parallel series of calculations based on apocalyptic numbers in the prophetic books, which also pointed to the significance of 1588.[31]

Tycho realized that the appearance of a new star was quite inconsistent with Aristotelian cosmology, and his conclusion, on the basis of its parallax, that the comet of 1577 was beyond the sphere of the moon, produced a second grave anomaly. He was already predisposed to accept the theory of matter of Paracelsus, and he realized that his new observations were completely consistent with the idea of Paracelsus that the cosmos existed in a state of dynamic change, subject to phases of growth and mutation. Tycho briefly discussed whether comets could be explained in terms of the favourite notion of Paracelsus that the heavens were populated by *penates*, which were the celestial equivalent of monstrous forms on earth, and fulfilled the idea of divine plenitude. As Christianson points out, it is significant that Tycho's observations were conducted in close association with Petrus Severinus, the leading Paracelsian of his age.[32]

In 1577, more than in 1572, Tycho drew astrological conclusions from his observations, predicting 'great alteration and reformation, both in the spiritual and secular regimes'. In particular he was struck by the observation that the conjunction of Saturn and Jupiter in Aries expected in 1603 was an event occurring once every 800 years, and therefore had happened only seven times since the beginning of the world. It could therefore be presumed that 'the eternal Sabbath of all Creation is at hand in this seventh maximum conjunction'.[33] The comet of 1577 accordingly led to Tycho's first serious commitment to the reform of the world system, and it alerted him to the idea that the end of the world and the establishment of a Golden Age could not be far distant. His tract on the 1577 comet was not published until the present century, but his prediction that the 'Seventh Revolution of the fiery Trigon' beginning in 1603 marked the inaugura- tion of a 'happier and more glorious state than ever before experienced in former ages' was repeated in Tycho's *Astronomiae instauratae progym- nasmata* (1602) and this prediction became a frequent point of reference in the course of the Thirty Years War and English Revolution.[34] It is probably more than a coincidence that the general idea of instauration propagated in the work by Brahe also became attached to the *Instauratio Magna*, the philosophical system of Francis Bacon, and in turn became the guiding theme for the intellectuals working to turn the English Revolution to Utopian purposes in line with expectations for the final age (see illustration 11, p. 51).

In essential respects there was little to separate Kepler and Paracelsus in their negative and positive reflections on astrology.[35] Kepler's platform for the reform of astrology, *De fundamentis astrologiae certioribus* (1601), followed very much the same lines as Paracelsus, and Kepler's later writ- ings showed no deviation from this position. He wrote on a much higher technical plane than Paracelsus, and in the course of his Neopythagorean constructions he saw greater potentialities for judicial astrology than ever seemed possible for Paracelsus. Acceptance as a normal part of physics of such devices as an animistic interpretation of the earth and celestial bodies, and the guiding concept of the *anima mundi*, rendered it easy to posit connections between the physical and organic and psychic worlds. Kepler, arguing along similar lines to Paracelsus, accepted that in addi- tion to regulating the normal course of events, God intervened in nature with signs such as new stars and comets which he believed should be accorded precisely the same significance as in the scriptures and among the ancients. Kepler absorbed the interest in comets of his teachers Brahe and Maestlin, and his writings on them extended from 1604 to 1625. Such signs addressed to man and the accompanying mutations on earth were regarded as proofs of God's grace, and of the absolute powers of God in His universe. Kepler used comets to justify the idea of divine plenitude and, also like Paracelsus, he connected them with spiritual beings in the cosmos. Kepler had no doubt that the political and cultural history of Christian Europe was closely geared to the cycles of cosmic events;

neither could celestial signs be regarded as fortuitous events without significance to human affairs. But the interpretation of such signs was recognized as a profoundly difficult exercise, necessitating reference to revealed as well as scientific sources. Comets were not so much regarded as heralds of specific events, as demonstrations of God's power in the universe and admonitions to all classes of mankind to prepare for imminent translation into another realm.[36] In *De stella nova* Kepler criticized aspects of Tycho's interpretation of the fiery Trigon, but recognized that the new star possessed a special cosmic and eschatological significance, heralding the climax of the divine plan. Dissensions among the Christians were regarded as a prelude to the conversion of the Indians in America and the Jews and Turks in the East.[37]

Kepler's horoscope for Wallenstein was by no means the last prepared for a great man, but few more were to emanate from famous astronomers.[38] Kepler's programme for the reform of astrology according to harmonic principles seems not to have convinced Thomas Harriot, and their contemporary Henry Briggs, the first Savilian Professor of Geometry, was also a sceptic, as were John Wilkins and his friends in the next generation at Oxford, whose views were in turn reflected in the Royal Society.[39] In France, Mersenne and Gassendi were persistent critics of astrology, while the philosophy of Descartes left little scope for miraculous intervention. All of this set the tone for the new age of science. The full potentialities of scientific investigation of the cosmos could be realized untrammelled by reference to prophecy and astrology. The records of the Royal Society, for instance, constitute a vast repository of information concerning the improvement in techniques of observation and the accumulation of data in the field of physical astronomy, presented almost completely without mention of extraneous factors. John Flamsteed, the first Astronomer Royal, and one of the main contributors to this process, accepted that astrology had provided his initiation into astronomy, but this art was abandoned once technical proficiency was assured.

The above remarks represent an appropriate end to the story and they seem to call for little further elucidation. It has been regarded as particularly significant of the lack of credit of astrology in scientific circles that active shows of criticism were not needed to prompt its demise.[40] This construction is however liable to a certain amount of correction. Astrology died neither promptly nor painlessly with the arrival of the new science.

Francis Bacon had accepted astrology quite as fully as Tycho and Kepler. The tract on the comet of 1618 by John Bainbridge, the first Savilian Professor of Astronomy, was completely traditional and it was employed for anti-Catholic and anti-Arminian propaganda.[41] Behind the scenes the Baconians were reconsidering their attitude to astrology. The sceptical consensus among the experts was less entire than might be thought. In 1648 William Petty proposed that the senior officer in his *Nosocomium academicum* should be primarily 'skilled in the best rules of judicial astrology, which he may apply to calculate the events of diseases, and prognosticate the weather; to the end that . . . the wheat may be separated from the chaff in that faculty likewise, and what is good therein may be applied to good uses, and the rest exploded'.[42] Petty's erstwhile friend, and eventual competitor for high office in Ireland, Benjamin Worsley, conducted an elaborate and lively defence of astrology against the 'Oxford professors', who were warned that their stubbornness on this issue would leave them in the near future with knowledge 'without Repute or Authority'.[43] Worsley regarded 'the doctrine of the Influence of those bodies, to be antient, a great, a usefull, a necessary, and a certaine truth, and such a truth as without the comprehension and right understanding of it noe man shall ever understand the Ancient philosophers, finde out their great secrets, or tincture, . . . nor performe anything considerable of it in Physicks'. He suspected that the influence of planets on earth was mediated by the moon.[44] In order to test this hypothesis Worsley, like Petty, gave high priority to the systematic investigation of all phenomena which might provide evidence of the coordination of celestial and terrestrial regularities.

The English Baconians thus devised a means whereby physical astrology could be subject to precise experimental enquiry. Many of the experts supported Worsley. They believed that this investigation was justified and were open-minded about its outcome. It is likely that the meteorological investigations conducted by Hooke, Towneley and a few others connected with the Royal Society represent the torso of the scheme proposed by Petty and Worsley during the Republic. Astrology possessed too many attractions and too much explanatory value to be sacrificed without reluctance. It was difficult to engage in effective religious and political polemic without the use of astrological imagery, and this imagery was all the more effective when inspired by conviction.

In England the Civil War, Republic, and Restoration were accompanied by an undiminishing tide of astrological commentary. Each turn of events was proclaimed as *annus mirabilis*. A review of the debate associated with a single event, the eclipse of 12 August 1654, reveals the participation of thirty-eight authors throughout Europe.[45] Gassendi's sceptical contribution to the discussion was sharply out of phase with the general concurrence on the astrological reading of this phenomenon. As on earlier occasions, prognostications occasionally scored some notable successes: William Lilly in 1651 and Richard Edlyn in 1663 predicted the

6. Reverse of commemorative medal, struck in 1666, of comet and fire of London.

plague for 1665 and fire for 1666. The year 1666 was as much surrounded by astrological, millennial and apocalyptic speculation as any date since 1500.[46] Lilly proclaimed that 'the English of all nations are most taken with prophecyes'; and England was described as a land of prophets by the French ambassador.[47] The establishment promoted the idea of a golden age under the new king, with the old republicans concentrating on the imagery of final confrontation with Antichrist. Thomas Sprat's *History of the Royal Society* (1667), and Dryden's poem *Annus Mirabilis* (1667), applied this astrological framework to their own apologetic advantage.[48] It should not be assumed that the identification of Charles II with messianic monarchy was regarded by contemporaries as the absurdity it appears with hindsight.[49]

The more persistent strain of astrology was tied up with prophecy, and was thus legitimated by a variety of biblical and non-biblical sources. Very few of the traditionally used sources of prophecy had fallen out of the picture by 1660. Most of the imagery then employed had been in use a hundred years earlier. There were also many examples of direct continuity. For instance, the prophecies of Paul Grebner, which were modelled on Paracelsus, produced in 1574, and presented shortly afterwards to Queen Elizabeth, were then deposited in the library of Trinity College, Cambridge, where they were frequently consulted by later commentators on prophetic texts, including Joseph Mede. These prophecies, like those of Tycho placing their emphasis on the mutations of the northern kingdoms, were taken as forecasting the English Revolution, the 'Novi Imperii Revolutio' destined to usher in an age of universal gladness, joy and delight. Grebner's pronouncements were thus invaluable for propaganda purposes during the Republic.[50]

The most skilful attempt at harmonizing biblical prophecy and astrology was made by Johann Heinrich Alsted, who discovered that Tycho's interpretation of the fiery Trigon coincided with his own attempts to convert the symbolism of Revelation into a precise chronology (see illustration 7, p.35). Alsted's ingenious use of two independent sources to forecast the future in precise mathematical terms exercised a profound influence throughout Europe, and perhaps particularly in Britain. In practical terms the distinguished Calvinist theologian gave firm support to the idea of a millennium, and he committed himself to 1694 as the date for its commencement. This date would mark the beginning of a period of universal peace and harmony, when the Jews and others would be finally converted.

Alsted's work signifies that the magic of prophecy had lost none of its force since the time of Paracelsus. Indeed the influence of prophecy was reinforced by the addition of three new elements: first, the centre of gravity of prophecy moved from non-scriptural sources to the books of Daniel and Revelation; secondly, the exegesis of these books was conducted according to a high level of technical proficiency and numerical exactness; thirdly, millenarianism was translated from the sectarian fringes to the respectable middle ground of protestant theology. As Beale aptly summed up: 'Mr. Dury retains a Notion of a great revolution and Restauration. And Alsted leads the stiffest Presbiters into a kind of Millenary expectation'.[51]

Alsted was not an isolated case. Napier of Merchiston applied his great mathematical gifts to deciphering the book of Revelation. A further major advance was made by Joseph Mede whose method of synchronisms unified the interpretation of the prophecies of Daniel and Revelation.

SPECULUM MUNDI.

RES MEMORABILES.

7. 'Speculum Mundi' from J.H. Alsted, *Thesaurus Chronologiae*.

Alsted's *Diatribe de mille annis apocalypticis* and Mede's *Clavis Apocalyptica*, both published in 1627, were translated, rendered into popular forms and voraciously plundered by popular writers at the outset of the Revolution.[52] But the revolutionary decades by no means exhausted interest in millennial prophecy. Especially at Cambridge Mede's work remained under continuous review, serving as a major source of inspiration first to More and Cudworth, then to Newton and Whiston. Between the time of Mede and that of Whiston the exegesis of the prophetic books attracted unflagging interest, and it is particularly notable that natural philosophers played a dominant role in this field. Not only the circle of Hartlib and the pansophists, but also the Platonists, Latitudinarians and early Newtonians were involved. At each stage the interpretation of the millennium was adapted for political purposes, whether by the Puritans to spur on their revolutionary effort, or by the Latitudinarians to promote resistance to James II and to justify the Glorious Revolution.[53]

Mede's contribution to the interpretation of the prophetic books was regarded as a triumph of analytical skill, and as a model for the scientific mentality of later generations. Newton's disciple Whiston described Mede as a man 'inspired for the interpretation of the Prophecies'. Newton himself acknowledged that 'Mr. Mede layd the foundation and I have built upon it: so I hope others will proceed higher untill the work be finished'. Any original contributor to this field was applauded as though reaching the peak of intellectual achievement. Thus More acclaimed Cudworth's lectures on the interpretation of Daniel as an event as important as the Copernican theory or the discovery of the circulation of blood.[54]

There was endless dispute concerning the definition of the millennium. No single vision of the millennial prophecies emerged as dominant. A variety of dates was canvassed regarding the onset of the millennium. More and Cradock favoured the older view that the final thousand years had begun with the Reformation. Hartlib and Dury had suggested 1655 and Thomas Goodwin 1666. Napier placed the Judgment between 1688 and 1700; Alsted proposed 1694 for the commencement of the millennium, while Whiston and Mede tentatively offered 1715 or 1716. Newton characteristically refused to be committed to any date in the near future. Whatever specific date was favoured, the scientists firmly believed that the ordained 6000-year span of life of the cosmos was ending and the way was being prepared for spiritual and possibly physical changes.

The byproducts of this revelation were many; for instance, the renewal of the crusading spirit opposed to Roman Catholicism because of the firm identification of this faith as the agent of Antichrist. Various manifesta-

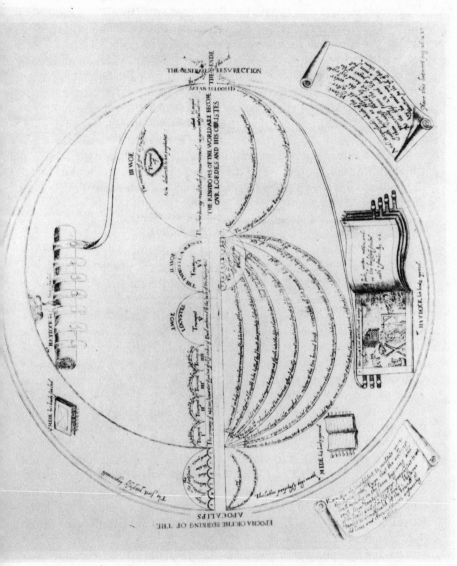

8.   'The Apocalyptik Type' from J. Mede, The Key of the Revelation.

tions of the imperialistic outlook among English scientists involving foreign and colonial commerce, missionary activities, and translation of the scriptures, should not be viewed simply as disinterested philanthropy or entrepreneurship on the part of the Christian virtuosi. The Indians of North America were regarded as particularly ripe candidates for conversion on the basis that they were likely to be the lost tribe of Israel. Even more concern was attracted to Jews among whom millenarianism was being stirred up by the wanderings of the charismatic Sabbatai Zevi.[55] Over the revolutionary decades the affairs of the Jews were carefully monitored for signs of their gathering in Israel, the transformation of Israel into a land of plenty, and the onset of the process of conversion. John Dury, one of the closest observers of the spiritual state of the Jews, believed that recent events recapitulated the miraculous experiences of Elijah on Mount Carmel when the 'clouds gathered, and with thunder they poured out such a flood of rain, that all the cisterns were filled and did run over'.[56]

Petrus Serrarius, a major source of information for the English on Sabbatianism, also acted as Oldenburg's agent in the Netherlands. *An Awakening Warning to the Wofull World* (1662) by Serrarius attracted widespread attention. This tract bore resemblances to the last desperate writings of the Fifth Monarchists produced at the time of the collapse of the Republic. It predicted that the planetary conjunction expected for late 1662 would be followed by the conversion of the Jews and the return of Jesus. Similarly radical millenarian ideas expressed by Jean de Labadie and Pierre Jurieu were widely diffused among English scientists during the following decades.[57] These associations might help to explain why Oldenburg as Secretary of the Royal Society came under political suspicion and suffered imprisonment at the hands of the agents of Charles II. Oldenburg's sympathetic interest in the Sabbatian cult continued, perhaps prompting Comenius to unearth the manuscript of his transparently millenarian *Via Lucis*, which he promptly dedicated to the Royal Society and transmitted to Oldenburg via Serrarius. It is therefore not quite such an anomaly that Comenius should aim at the Royal Society a work framed to inspire his pansophist sympathizers at the outset of the English Revolution. In the course of discussions among members of the Royal Society concerning the expectation of the Jubilee, Beale offered the thought that a telling manifestation of the final age would be 'that knowledge will abound largely over all the world: And I fix upon your Society as the Cynosure'.[58]

The idea of the integration of the data of biblical chronology and astronomy proved to be the beginning of a comprehensive attempt at reconciliation of the scriptures and science. The genre of physico-theology

9.   Comenius, Frontispiece Emblem from *Didactica Opera Omnia*.

launched in the second half of the seventeenth century has primarily
attracted attention by virtue of its relevance to the natural theology tradition. The physico-theologies are also seen as an explaining-away of supposedly miraculous phenomena, thereby further extending the *de facto*
authority of the sciences against religion. The more general and popular
handbooks by authors like Derham inspire such interpretations. But
examination of the growth of the literature shows that one of the major
concerns was to provide further justification of biblical chronology. The
naturalists conducted a celebrated debate over the nature of fossils, some
favouring their organic origin, others their formation under the aegis of
some kind of plastic principle. These differences were part of the wider
dispute over the universal deluge, and the universal deluge itself was
regarded as a crucial issue, not for reasons of curiosity, but because it was

believed to be the Old Testament analogue of the imminent conflagration thought by many to mark the onset of the millennium.[59] By the later seventeenth century, the experimental philosophers knew enough about explosives, volcanoes, earthquakes, and mechanics to be able to frighten themselves and their public with various models of possible future catastrophes.

The first daring attempt at a 'universal history' from the creation to the millennium, synthesising the evidence of 'Scripture, Reason and ancient Tradition' was Thomas Burnet's *Sacred Theory of the Earth*. This went through three Latin and eight English editions between 1681 and 1759, assuming in that age much of the earlier popularity of Mede and Alsted. Burnet employed Cartesian physics to explain the mutation of the perfect egg-shaped earth formed at the creation, into the imperfect globe left by the flood. The misshapen and inflammable earth would be returned to a more perfect form by the future conflagration. The notion of the literal truth of universal conflagration had already been sanctioned by Henry More.[60] Following the version by Burnet, this idea was widely supported.

Joseph Glanvill presented a terrifying prospect of the earth being enveloped in a ball of fire which would then drift away and become a wandering comet.[61] John Evelyn, long interested in earthquakes and chemical explosions, gave an account of the translation of the saints into clouds before the 'dreadfull Conflagration of this present Earth, which shall now be burnt up, and so refin'd as to be made a New Earth'. He believed that the terraqueous globe was likely to explode in the manner of a 'grenado about our ears'.[62] As Margaret Jacob has demonstrated the threat of imminent physical catastrophe was used by the Latitudinarians as a political weapon in their own favour.[63]

Despite the ever-increasing knowledge concerning their physical characteristics and motions, comets lost none of their explanatory place in the universal histories. Against the background of investigations into comets at the Royal Society, John Beale prepared for John Evelyn a detailed statement of the correspondences between comets and political or economic fluctuations, which was probably initiated because the comets of 1664 and 1665 were blamed for the catastrophes of the plague and fire.[64] Such correspondences were difficult to ignore. John Edwards, the highly respected puritan divine of Cambridge, dedicated to Seth Ward a general review of expert opinion relating to comets. Ward had himself written on comets and he was one of the Oxford academics known to be cool towards astrology. Edwards attacked judicial astrology with vehemence, but he accepted that political and natural events were 'chained together like Natural Causes and Effects'. Comets were regarded as signs of God's intentions. Of special current concern, the 'astonishing Comet of 1680 . . . shall be of universal Influence, and many Nations shall share in the Revolution and Occurrences which it shall produce'.[65] The comets of 1680/1 and 1682 generated the customary flurry of speculations. Lilly regarded the comet of 1680/1 as a portent of his own death. He obligingly died in the following year at the age of eighty. Ashmole described the comet of 1680/1 as a 'terrible' portent threatening plague and famine, and he communicated three German tracts on this comet to the Royal Society.[66] Ezerel Tong, Hartlib's old associate, who combined botanical writing for the Royal Society with cloak-and-dagger operations against Catholics which earned him notoriety in the Titus Oates affair, mobilized the prophecies of Tycho and Grebner to give a messianic meaning to the comet of 1680/1.[67] In view of evidence of this kind it is doubtful whether we are justified in asserting that the change of worldview associated with Latitudinarianism had left no 'room for the stars as instruments of such intervention' in human affairs by the deity.[68]

Before 1680 every conceivable kind of trajectory had been canvassed for comets. Observations on the comets of 1680/1 and 1682 provided the data upon which Halley worked in framing his theory that comets moved in the same kind of elliptical orbits as planets. As mentioned above Halley's comet of 1682 was the comet giving rise to the speculations of Paracelsus in 1531. The idea of the orbital motion of comets was also important for Newton and it was quickly turned to wider purposes. Newton was consulted on the sidelines as a squabble developed between Halley and Whiston concerning the latter's hypothesis, deriving from the 1680/1 comet, that the 'confused Mass of Air, and irregular Streams from the Comet's Atmosphere or Tail might afford a fair Solution of that Phenomenon [the deluge]'. This was the 'New Theory' to which Whiston became passionately attached.[69] On the basis of Newtonian principles and scriptural chronology, Whiston in his *New Theory of the Earth* (1696) argued that a comet was not only the likely cause of the obliquity of the earth to the ecliptic, but also that the comet of 1680/1 was the actual cause of the deluge. The final conflagration would be caused by another intervention of a comet, this time directly striking the combustible earth. Whiston thus improved on Burnet and produced an explanation for the major parameters of universal history consistent with the economy of explanation so congenial to the Newtonians. Not to be outdone Halley himself delivered a paper to the Royal Society discussing the possibility of the earth being struck by a comet. Whiston regarded his scheme as confirmation of the working of extraordinary providence, the 'most spectacular and strange Effect of the most wise and sagacious Providence of God in his mighty Revelation'.[70]

Whiston's *New Theory* was dedicated to Newton and the latter was of course conversant with the whole debate in which Whiston was involved, from the moment of the publication of the first edition of Burnet's book. Whiston cited Newton's support against allegorical interpretations of 'days' of the prophetic books in the interests of preserving the traditional chronology.[71] Newton shared Whiston's views on the accessibility of the prophetic books, but seems to have agreed with Edwards that the idea of a universal conflagration and the 'Notion of a New material Earth and New Set of heavenly Bodies for Men to inhabit in, is all Romance and Fiction'.[72] Newton's own ideas on comets were less obviously dramatic than those of his disciple Whiston. Nevertheless they both believed that comets must play some positive functional role in the cosmic process. Newton discovered in comets an ideal source of materials to prevent the running down of the regenerative processes of the earth. Thus by means of the agency of comets God was involved in the perpetual renovation of the world, as well as preparing for its final restoration at the Last Judgment.[73] Whether Newton believed in more adventurous speculations concerning comets, depends on our evaluation of the worth of the enigmatic Conduitt memorandum.[74]

The physico-theologies embodied their own style of interpretation of universal history, tending to deflect attention from the immediate future and local events towards the final general cataclysm and restitution. The scientific language belonged to Cartesianism and Newtonianism, but the underlying ethos indicates continuity with a prophetic tradition coextensive with the Scientific Revolution. The scientists thus perpetuated the idea of the control over man's destiny by the 'supreme Monarch . . . with an irresistible and boundless power and dominion'. Or, as Whiston expressed it: 'Nature is God's Constitution, and ever subservient to him; and the State of the Natural is always accommodated to that of the Moral World'.[75] Among Newton's contemporaries there was a prevailing sense that the revolution of knowledge and unsealing of the prophetic books were two aspects of the revelation of God's intentions for man during the universal restoration of the world. John Ray pointed to an unquenchable curiosity about 'the fates of Kingdoms and Commonwealth, especially the Periodic Mutations, and final Catastrophe of the World', which linked his contemporaries with the divination practices of colleges or schools of wisemen, magicians, astrologers, and soothsayers of the ancient world.[76] There was also continuing faith not only among the Platonists, but also with Stillingfleet, Whiston and Newton that there existed a fundamental unity between prophecies of the scriptures and those contained in the hermetic writings, Sybilline oracles and other works of ancient theology.[77]

NOTES

1. John Webster, *The Displaying of Witchcraft* (London, 1677), p.183. For background see F. Oakley (1961), Christian Theology and the Newtonian Science: The Rise of the Concept of the Laws of Nature, *Church History*, **30**, 433–57.

2. Theophrast von Hohenheim, gen. Paracelsus, *Sämtliche Werke: I Abteilung, Medizinische, naturwissenschaftliche und philosophische Schriften*, ed. K. Sudhoff, 14 vols (Munich/Berlin, 1922–33), hereafter 'PI'; *2 Abteilung, Theologische und religionsphilosophische Schriften*, ed. K. Goldammer (Wiesbaden, 1955–), hereafter 'PII'. *Auslegung zum Leichtenberger*, PI, **8**, 511–14; *De Eclipsi Solis*, PI, **8**, 225–30; *Practica auf Europen*, PI, **7**, 455–62.

3. G. Hellmann (1914), Aus der Blützeit der Astrometeorologie, *Beiträge zur Geschichte der Meteorologie*, **1**, 5–102; L. Thorndike, *A History of Magic and Experimental Science*, vol. **5** (New York, 1941), pp.178–233. J. Friedrich, *Astrologie und Reformation oder die Astrologen als Prediger und Urheber des Bauenkriegs* (Munich, 1864); A. Warburg, *Heidenisch-antike Weissagung in Wort und Bild zu Luthers Zeiten* (Heidelberg, 1920); R.S. Westman (1980), The astronomer's role in the sixteenth century: a preliminary survey, *History of Science*, **18**, 105–47 for a useful background survey.

4. Thorndike, p.131; P. Zambelli (1965), ed., Cornelio Agrippa: scritti inediti e dispersi, *Rinascimento*, **16**, Second Series, v.

5. Zambelli, pp.169–70. See also *idem* (1976), Magic and radical reformation in Agrippa of Nettesheim, *Journal of the Warburg and Courtauld Institutes*, **39**, 69–103.

6. Johannes Indagine, *Introductiones Apotelesmaticae elegantes* (Frankfurt, 1522). F. Hermann (1934), Johannes Indagine, *Archiv für hessische Geschichte und Altertumskunde*, **18**, 274–91.

7. C. Ginzburg, *Il nicodemismo* (Turin, 1970), pp.10–11.

8. Ginzburg, pp.29–43.

9. Brunfels, *Almanach von dem XXVI Jar an bitz zü Endt der Welt aller Welt* (Strasbourg, 1526).

10. G.H. Williams, *The Radical Reformation* (London, 1962), pp.261–2. See illustration 3 (p.20).

11. *Astronomia Magna*, PI, **12**, 283–4.

12. *Astronomia Magna*, PI, **12**, 284–5. See also *Auslegung der Papstbilder*, PI, **12**, 511–14; *Practica auf Europen*, PI, **8**, 237–53.

13. *Astronomia Magna*, PI, **12**, 318, 320–1.

14. *Volumen Paramirum*, PI, **1**, 181.

15. *Auslegung über die zehen gebott gottes*, PII, **7**, 119; K.-H. Weimann, Eine neu aufgefundene Paracelsus-Handschrift, in S. Domandl, ed., *Paracelsus Werk und Wirkung: Festgabe für K. Goldammer zum 60. Geburtstag* (Vienna, 1975), pp.353–61; p.355.

16. D.Kurze, *Johannes Lichtenberger (†1503). Ein Studie zur Geschichte der Prophetie und Astrologie* (Historische Studien Heft 397, Lübeck/Hamburg, 1960); M Reeves, *The Influence of Prophecy in the Later Middle Ages* (Oxford, 1979), pp. 347–51.

17. Kurze, pp.46–52.

18. Kurze, pp.57–62.

19. Kurze, pp.62–6.

20. *Auslegung zum Liechtenberger*, PI, **7**, 477–530.

21. G Seebas, *Das reformatorische Werk des Andreas Osiander* (Nuremberg, 1967); *idem, Bibliographia Osiandrica* (Nieuwkoop, 1971); B. Wrightman, Andreas Osiander's contribution to the Copernican achievement, in R.S. Westman, ed., *The Copernican Achievement* (Los Angeles, 1975), pp.213–43.

22. *Auslegung der Papstbilder*, PI, **12**, 509–85.

23. *Die Prognostikation auf 24 zukünftige Jahre*, PI, **10**, 580–620; pp.580–3.

24. *Auslegung des Cometen 1531*, PI, **9**, 373–91. See illustration 4 (p.25). This comet was the first to be commemorated in a broadsheet, and the first in the modern era to be subject to intense astronomical observation.

25. G.R. Potter, *Zwingli* (Cambridge, 1976), pp.390-419.

26. Webster, Alchemical and Paracelsian medicine, pp. 326, 328; Stephen Batemann, ed., *Joyful News out of Helvetia* [London, 1575].

27. R. Grant, *A History of Physical Astronomy* (London, 1852), p.292.

28. E. Panofsky, *The Life and Art of Albrecht Dürer* (Princeton, 1955), p.162. See illustration 5 (p.28). For a rival view, see D. Pingree (1980), A new look at 'Melencolia I', *Journal of the Warburg and Courtauld Institutes*, **43**, 257–8.

29. C.D. Hellman, *The Comet of 1577: Its Place in the History of Astronomy* (New York, 1944), p.103.

30. Tycho Brahe, *Opera Omnia*, **1**, 30–4.

31. G. Mattingly, *The Defeat of the Armada* (London, 1959), p.160.

32. Brahe, *Opera Omnia*, **4**, 381–96; J.R. Christianson (1979), Tycho Brahe's treatise on the comet of 1577, *Isis*, **70**, 110–40.

33. Christianson, pp.137–40; Hellman, *The Comet of 1577*, pp.118–36.

34. Brahe, *Opera Omnia*, **3**, 311–19. See also pp. 293, 307, for references to Paracelsus.

35. G. Simon, *Kepler astronome astrologue* (Paris, 1979), pp.27–130; C.D. Hellman (1975), Kepler and comets, *Vistas in Astronomy*, **18**, 789–96; R.S. Westman (1972), The comet and the cosmos: Kepler, Mästlin and the Copernican hypothesis, *Studia Copernicana*, **5**, 7–30.

36. Kepler, *De Cometis libelli tres* (1619–1620), *Gesammelte Werke*, **8**, 259–62.

37. Kepler, *De stella nova* (1606), *Gesammelte Werke*, **1**, 349–50.

38. Kepler, *Opera Omnia*, 8 vols, ed. C. Frisch (Frankfurt and Erlangen, 1858–70), **1**, 387; G. Mann, *Wallenstein* (London, 1976), pp. 76–80 and *passim*.

39. Kepler, *Gesammelte Werke*, **15**, 349–50. K. Thomas, *Religion and the Decline of Magic* (London, 1971), pp.351–2, for a sound review of the English critics.

40. B. Capp, *Astrology and the Popular Press: English Almanacs 1500–1800* (London, 1979), p.278.

41. John Bainbridge, *An Astronomicall Description of the Late Comet* (London, 1619).

42. William Petty, *The Advice of W.P. to Mr. Samuel Hartlib. For the Advancement of some particular Parts of Learning* (London, 1647), p.12.

43. Worsley's tract was translated into Latin by Nicolas Mercator and circulated widely: in England to Ashmole, Beale, Boyle, John Sadler, John Sparrow, and Thomas Street, and abroad to Hevelius, Joachim Hübner, Joachim Jungius. Most of these seem to have supported Worsley. Beale to Hartlib, 14 December 1658, commented that he 'never saw Astrology more tenderly represented nor more fully demonstrated than in his discourse', Sheffield University, Hartlib Papers LII. See also Hartlib-Boyle, 8 December 1657, Boyle, *Works,* 6, 97.

44. 'Mr. Worsly's Physico-Astrological Letter' (20 October 1657) and 'Problemata Physico-Astrologicum', Hartlib Papers XLII.

45. E. Labrousse, *L'Entrée de Saturne au Lion. L'Éclipse de Soleil du 12 Août 1654* (The Hague, 1974).

46. D. Brady (1979), 1666: the year of the beast, *Bulletin of the John Rylands University Library of Manchester,* **61**, 314–336. See illustration 6 (p.33).

47. R. McKeon, *Politics and Poetry in Restoration England: The Case of Dryden's 'Annus Mirabilis'* (Cambridge, Mass., 1975), p.205; Lilly to Ashmole, 12 February 1666, *Ashmole* (no.66 below), **3**, 1050.

48. McKeon, *Politics and Poetry.*

49. Capp, *Astrology and the Popular Press*, p.173. See below, chapter 3, no.52.

50. *A Prophecy of Paul Grebnerus* (London, 1649). [William Lilly], *A brief description of the future history of Europe from 1650 to 1710* (London, 1650); Lilly, *Monarchy or No Monarchy in England* (London, 1651). For Mede's consultation of the Grebner prophecies, see Mede to Hartlib, 3 April 1638, *Works,* ed. J. Worthington, 2 vols (London, 1672), **2**, 1077–8.

51. Beale to Evelyn, 15 March 1668, Christ Church, Oxford, Evelyn Letters A–B, f.70.

52. For general reviews see B.W. Ball, *A Great Expectation: Eschatological Thought in English Protestantism to 1660* (London, 1975); B. Capp, *The Fifth Monarchy Men* (London, 1972); K.R. Firth, *The Apocalyptic Tradition in Reformation Britain 1530-1645* (Oxford, 1979). See illustrations 7 and 8 (pp.35 and 37). For Newton's edition of Alsted's *Thesaurus chronologiae*, see Harrison, *Library of Newton*, p.85.

53. Webster, *The Great Instauration;* M.C. Jacob, *The Newtonians and the English Revolution 1689–1720* (Hassocks, 1976).

54. Whiston, *Essay on the Revelation of St. John*, 2nd edn (London, 1744), p.107. Newton, Treatise on Revelation, ed. Manuel, *Religion of Newton*, Appendix A, p.121. More, *An Exposition of the Grand Mystery of Godliness* (London, 1660), p.xvi.

55. G. Scholem, *Major Trends in Jewish Mysticism* (New York, 1946), pp.286–324; *idem, Sabbatai Sevi, the Mystical Messiah, 1626–1676* (Princeton, N.J., 1973); McKeon, *Politics and Poetry*, pp.206–8 and *passim.*

56. [John Dury], *An Information concerning the Present State of the Jewish Nation in Europe and Judea* (London, 1658), p.220. See illustration 9 (p.39).

57. Jean de Labadie, *Le Héraut du Grand Roy Jesus* (Amsterdam, 1667); Pierre Jurieu, *L'Accomplissement des Prophéties* (Rotterdam, 1686). John Locke, *Correspondence*, ed. E.S. De Beer, 8 vols (Oxford, 1976–), 2, 620, 632. John Worthington, *Diary and Correspondence,* ed. J. Crossley, 3 vols (Chetham Soc., Manchester, 1847–86), 2, 108. Henry Oldenburg, *Correspondence*, ed. A.R. & M.B. Hall (Madison, etc., 1965-), 1, 123–5; 3, 446–7; 4, 388–9. J. van den Berg, The eschatological expectation of seventeenth century Dutch protestantism with regard to the Jewish people, in P. Toon, ed., *Puritans, The Millennium and the Future of Israel* (Cambridge, 1970), pp.137–53. McKeon, *Politics and Poetry*, pp.196, 201, 225.

58. Beale to Evelyn, 15 March 1668, Evelyn Letters A–B, f.70.

59. For reviews from various angles see: C.E. Raven, *John Ray Naturalist* (Cambridge, 1950), pp.419–30; J.M. Levine, *Dr. Woodward's Shield* (Berkeley and Los Angeles, 1977); R. Porter, *The Making of Geology: Earth Science in Britain 1660-1815* (Cambridge, 1977), pp.32–90.

60. More, *Grand Mystery of Godliness*, pp.230–3.

61. Glanvill, *Lux orientalis* (London, 1682), pp.137–41. Harrison, *Library of Newton*, p.184.

62. Evelyn, Concerning the millennium (1688), Christ Church, Oxford, Evelyn Manuscripts 35, 2r-v. See also Evelyn to Tenison, 15 October 1692, *Diary and Correspondence*, ed. W. Bray, 4 vols (London, 1859), 4, 325–30.

63. Jacob, *Newtonians*, pp.100–42; M.C. Jacob and W.A. Lockwood (1972), Political millenarianism and Burnet's sacred theory, *Science Studies*, 2, 265–79.

64. Beale, 'A Briefe of Comets' (c.1666), Evelyn Letters A–B, ff.24–6. See also Beale to Boyle, 30 October 1670, Boyle, *Works*, 6, 429–30, where Beale notes that Mede valued dreams as a means to unlocking the mysteries of the scriptures. See illustration 6 (p.33).

65. [John Edwards], *Cometomantia. A Discourse of Comets* [London, 1684], pp.72–3, 164.

66. C.H. Josten, ed., *Elias Ashmole*, 5 vols (Oxford, 1966), 4, 1677, 1681, 1687, 1701.

67. Tong, *The Northern Star* (London, 1680).

68. Capp, *Astrology and the Popular Press*, p.280. At the expert level the total scepticism of Hooke (*Posthumous Works*, ed. R. Waller, London, 1705, p.165) contrasts with unambiguous affirmation of the relevance of comets to prophecy by John Whiston, *Memoirs*, 2 vols (London, 1753), 2, 131–3.

69. Whiston, *A Vindication of the New Theory of the Earth* (London, 1698), Preface. See Porter, pp.74–8 for a brief review of explanations of the deluge. Harrison, *Library of Newton*, p.262.

70. Whiston, *New Theory of the Earth*, pp.357–8; Jacob, *Newtonians*, pp.135–6.

71. Newton to Burnet, *Correspondence*, ed. H.W. Turnbull *et al.*, 7 vols (Cambridge, 1959–77), 2, 329–34; Whiston, *Vindication of the New Theory*, Preface; *idem, Memoirs*, 1, 35–8, 94. Manuel, *Religion of Newton*, p.83.

72. Edwards, *A Compleat History of All the Dispensations and Methods of Religion*, 2 vols (London, 1699), 2, 899; Newton, Of the day of judgment, in Manuel, *Religion of Newton*, Appendix B, p.132.

73. D. Kubrin (1967), Newton and the cyclical cosmos: providence and the mechanical philosophy, *Journal of the History of Ideas,* **28**, 325–46, for a suggestive preliminary view; R.S. Westfall, *Never at Rest. A Biography of Isaac Newton* (Cambridge, 1980), pp.390–7.

74. Westfall, *Never At Rest*, p.862.

75. Newton, The end of the world, in Manuel, *Religion of Newton*, p.104, consistent with William Allen, *Of the State of the Church in Future Ages* (London, 1684). See also Manuel, pp.61–3. Whiston, *New Theory*, p.361.

76. John Ray, *Miscellaneous Discourses concerning the Dissolution and Changes of the World*, 3rd edn (London, 1713), pp.296–7.

77. Whiston, *Astronomical Principles of Religion*, 2nd edn (London, 1725), p.289. See also Whiston, *A Vindication of the Sybylline Oracles* (1715), and *The Literal Accomplishment of Scripture Prophecies* (1724).

3   SPIRITUAL MAGIC

The cosmologies of the ages of Paracelsus and Newton were deeply influenced by the sense that our planetary system was not only unlikely to persist in its present form, but also that its end might come about in the near future. To Paracelsus the last days seemed imminent, whereas in the Augustan age the end seemed less near, but still close enough to provoke committed debate in the highest intellectual circles. In the intervening period this problem was never far from view, its prominence tending to reflect the prevailing level of political and religious instability and social unrest. Whatever the degree of urgency, the generally accepted conclusion among all parties that the Reformation marked a crucial stage in, if not the onset of, the final struggle with Antichrist, aroused strong feelings of anxiety and pessimism. Prognostications, chronologies and increasingly realistic and convincing speculative models emanating from well-informed scientific sources, must have contributed to the sense of expectation. By comparison, any loss of sense of coherence occasioned by the transition from a geocentric to heliocentric cosmology was altogether insignificant.

To counteract any sense of irredeemable pessimism or disorientation occasioned by the above speculations each communion or denomination looked towards its own final ascendancy by the time of the final Judgment. As a parallel trend in the secular sphere the scientist held out prospects of ultimate material amelioration. Thus the phenomenon was saved; intellectual energies and scientific ingenuity could be legitimately devoted to elaborating terms for the restoration of an earthly paradise.

The hermeneutic efforts of scientists were often inexplicit or intentionally imprecise when dealing with some of the more theologically contentious aspects of eschatology. Paracelsus and the Newtonians just managed to steer clear of the extreme Anabaptist and Huguenot millenarians respectively. But they contributed to the idea that the elect would enjoy a prolonged period of earthly bliss either before or after the Judgment. A construction of this kind permitted maximum opportunity for the exploitation of the idea of secular progress based on the growth of science. Consequently, throughout the Scientific Revolution, Christian eschatology provided an undiminishing incentive towards science, if not a primary motivating factor.

In the course of the Scientific Revolution the idea of recovery from the adverse effects of the fall and restitution of man's dominion over nature contained in Christian eschatology was reinforced by an analogous set of ideas inherited from ancient theology. The more magical Neoplatonic writings and the Corpus Hermeticum made current by the Florentine Neoplatonists, contained more than a veiled expectation that initiates of hermeticism would ascend to a level of mystical illumination offering a variety of benefits, including the possibility of being transformed into powerful Magi. As Pagel, Rossi, Walker, and Yates have pointed out, the aspirations of experimental science were intimately entangled with the fortunes of the Renaissance Magus.[1] Both experimental science and natural magic were involved in the understanding and conquest of the forces associated with spiritual magic. The latter is construed as the non-demonic form of magic utilizing the powers of the *spiritus mundi*, and reaching no higher in its mediations than the human spirit. Natural magic or science could thus be viewed not only as a manifestation of skill or knowledge, but also as a sign of election and as a reward for the elect.

At very few points in his writings did Paracelsus fail to relate his subject matter to the origin and destiny of things. His ideas on life and matter are rooted in his interpretation of the opening verses of Genesis. Paracelsus expressed himself variously on eschatology, reflecting on occasions most of the points of view known within the Christian church.[2] Sometimes he placed emphasis on the prospects for Christ's imminent return. The frequent appearance of comets in particular, and the increasing instability of the times, whether climatically or politically, seemed to point towards this end. The world seemed to be running down, to have reached its last stage of life. The logical outcome was thus a cosmic catastrophe and the initiation of a new world of the spirit after the shattering of the old material world.[3]

However, for the most part he placed an emphasis on the enduring nature of the trial of mankind mounted by God during the last Monarchy on earth, giving man the fullest opportunity to accept salvation, to be raised to the highest degree above the level of animals and beyond control of the stars.[4] It was therefore more important to seek the rule of God than to engage in vain prophecies.[5] It was granted to man to know what would occur, but not when. Paracelsus preached against those desperate folk who were predicting the end of the world and warned that we had no idea how many generations would elapse before the final outcome.[6] His remarks carry the obvious implication that the Christian was not justified in abandoning his longer-term responsibilities on the assumption of an immediate break-up of the present order.

Paracelsus equalled any renaissance optimist in his views on the dignity and capacities of man. Man was cast in the image of God; he was the

10.   From Paracelsus, *Prognostication auff XXIIII Jahr Zukünfftig.*

centre part of creation, the summation of all the elements in the macro-cosm. His status was so high and so great that he is provided with *arcana*, *mysteria* and *magnalia* without number from the heavens.[7] As God's legitimate heir, the effects of the Fall notwithstanding, man was destined to inherit the kingdom on earth.[8] The Devil would stand in the way of this inheritance, and attempt to prevent man from transcending his earthbound nature. But man would attain this definite goal or 'number' and achieve perfection, so signifying the return of paradise and final victory over the Devil.[9] The circle of the world would then be completed, with man established at a position of supremacy in its centre.[10]

It might be anticipated that at this point Paracelsus would declare for the breaking up of the present order of things. However he allowed for an indefinite boundary and even for an extensive interval between the last phase of world and the future state of the resurrection. Thus paradise might spill over even into the present monarchy, so creating a period during which the elect would enjoy the benefits of both forms of existence. A golden age or New Hebron (Eden) would be established on earth. His writings strongly implied that the transition towards the earthly paradise had already begun.[11]

11. Title page, Francis Bacon, *Novum Organum*.

Paracelsus believed that from a practical point of view man would only learn to exploit nature to its fullest extent if he were to learn by the mistakes of the past. God had granted all men since the Fall the capacity to overcome their disadvantages and perfect their arts and sciences. By following the light of nature, those capacities, implanted in man like a seed, could be developed to perfection. Nature was so organized that all things were arranged in a 'concordance', shared out on earth according to human needs, and awaiting initiative for the development of all necessary crafts and industries.[12]

God had provided all monarchies with a perfect light of nature, but this light had been exploited very unevenly and inadequately by past generations. The people had falsely believed that new arts were the product of the heavens and they had fatalistically resigned themselves to being subjugated by nature. They had not learned from the example of Solomon and other patriarchs and prophets that wisdom came from God: only those who subjected themselves to the reign of God would achieve full realization of their capacities. The sciences had made a promising start among the sages of the east, ending with Hippocrates, who were truly pious men, being rewarded with great mysteries and *magnalia*; but Plato and Aristotle fell under a dark cloud, their imitators in subsequent times achieving rhetorical effect without the backing of substance. Learned men were like parrots, men with bent beaks and clumsy feet, crowing and singing the songs of all birds, producing impressive-looking books, but of dead print containing only eloquence, ornament and superficial splendour. Their song was no better than the clattering of a stork or the chattering of a magpie.[13]

Apart from regarding the moral example of the sages, practitioners of the sciences and arts could learn nothing from the past. They should look forward to a new age. Besides, their own times or monarchy presented hitherto unparalleled problems, owing to the pressure of population and the scientific and medical needs of an advanced society. Books written two thousand years ago for an entirely different culture could scarcely be relevant to this situation.[14]

But there was no reason for lack of optimism. The latest ages were predestined to see the greatest achievement, by virtue of the predestined intellectual rebirth. The nearer man's approach to Judgment Day the greater would be the development of his learning, acuteness, wisdom and reason.[15] For these reasons Paracelsus felt justified in breaking with tradition in order to develop a form of science and medicine consistent with the needs of the last monarchy, and durable until the dawning of the final age. Although little as yet seemed to have been achieved it was God's will respecting the immediate future that we should have experience of all of

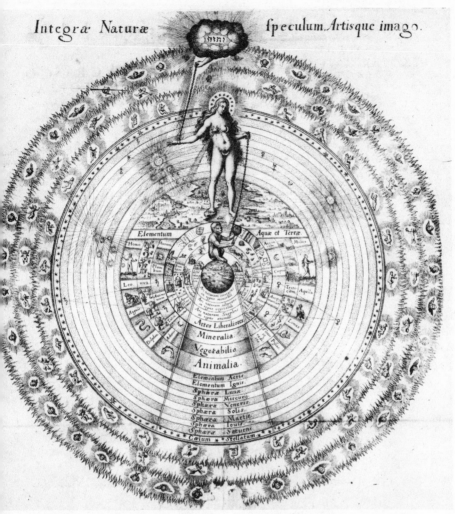

12. From R. Fludd, *Utriusque cosmi . . . metaphysica.*

his works, and come to possess knowledge of all the secrets of nature,
with nothing being withheld. There would be revealed to mankind great
and wonderful arts and improvements, and civilisation would achieve an
unprecedented understanding of the firmament, sea and earth. Gradually
the quality of life would improve; the seasons and weather would be
favourable; the land would be fruitful and the harvests rich; animals and
man would prosper; disease and misfortune would vanish.[16]

None of this was very different from the imagery of the New Jerusalem
prevalent in the early church, and cultivated in prophecies from Papias

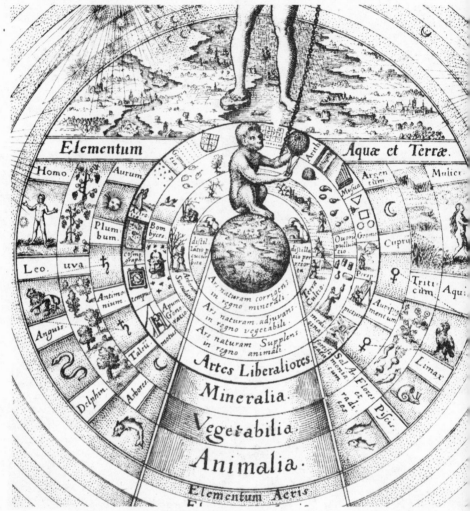

13.   Detail from Fludd, *Utriusque*.

onwards, and which surfaced periodically during phases of millenarianism. Each revival placed the emphasis slightly differently. For obvious reasons of advantage the millenarianism of the generation of Paracelsus, exploited extensively by the radical sects, placed its emphasis on the overthrow of the civil and ecclesiastical establishment, with the substitution of a fellowship of the poor, bound together by ties of mutual service and sharing of property. Paracelsus keenly advocated this platform both in its negative and positive aspects. His assault on the values of the medical establishment merely betokened an application to a special case of his feelings concerning the learned professions and the princely courts. On the other hand his respect for the usefulness of folk medicine reflects his acknowledgment of the basic virtue of simple people. Exaltation of the poor to the detriment of the rich is a theme introduced by Paracelsus at many points in his scientific and religious writings. The missing ingredient compared with other preachers developing the same theme is the sense of any desire to affiliate with any sect or specific religious movement. Like certain other spiritual reformers such as Sebastian Franck and Caspar Schwenckfeld, Paracelsus steered away from groups such as the Anabaptists. Indeed he regarded all sectarian groups, whether supporters of Luther, Huss, Calvin, Zwingli, Bucer, Schwenckfeld, or the Anabaptists, as detracting from the ideal of a unified spiritual church.[17]

The social ethic adopted by Paracelsus strongly influenced his ideas for the mapping out of the future course for intellectual progress. Nothing would be achieved in the degenerate world of the scholar. His own restless wanderings had taught him that the model for productive knowledge was provided by the best practices of the manual arts. It was the humble practitioners in these areas who were exposing the full extent of the treasures of nature and exploiting them to the best advantage.

Only by travelling, and systematically and minutely studying the diversity of things would the true extent of the variety of diseases, living organisms, or minerals be revealed. The chemist could not expect the mountains to come to him; he must visit them and there study the metallurgical and chemical methods of the workmen. It would then immediately be realized that species within any group, whether diseases or minerals, were infinitely more numerous than had been anticipated by the learned commentators. The traveller would also learn what seemed to be overlooked by the medieval compilers, that species and diseases were localized phenomena, Providence having provided in any one locality and for any one nation, everything required for material needs. This adaptation of the design argument was used to cut the ground from under classical sources, which even at their best, Paracelsus urged, were remote from the experience of the northern peoples.[18]

Paracelsus was giving forceful expression to an instinct which was rapidly spreading among his contemporaries and particularly among his compatriots. There was growing impatience and doubt concerning the scientific usefulness of current fashionable compilations such as *Gart der Gesundheit*, *Hortus Sanitatus*, and Rösslin's *Kreuterbuch*, all of which claimed distinction on grounds of derivation from classical and Arabic sources.[19] The investigative instincts and intense naturalistic detail awoken in Dürer at the turn of the century, were passed on to his disciples and imitators. They in turn worked with such authors as Brunfels, Fuchs, Bock, Gesner, and Agricola, whose works transformed the level of commentary on the plants, animals, minerals and technology of Europe, and paved the way for the various types of investigative natural history produced during the next century.

Paracelsus himself made no direct contribution to this systematic effort. Even those of his writings which might have lent themselves to the listing of types tend to drift off in other directions. Nevertheless a vast amount of authentic data concerning chemistry, pharmacology and other aspects of medicine is buried in his writings, much of it judged by lexicographers and historians of the specialized sciences to constitute pioneering recording or observation.

Perhaps the exhaustive analysis of the older literature and organization of data which appealed to such encyclopaedic mentalities as Conrad Gesner, seemed to Paracelsus like a secondary priority. He was more concerned with the effective exploitation of the properties of commonly-available materials and with the understanding of the dynamics of natural processes, normal and pathological. By analogy with the sophisticated routines of the mineral workers, and in expectation of regaining the arcana of the ancient *magi*, Paracelsus placed his emphasis on argument by analogy, acute observation and the revelation of new properties by experimental manipulation.

Paracelsus argued that the light which provided the path to grace, was also the light of nature given to guide man to the *secreta*, *mysteria* and *magnalia*, which were offered as rewards to those accepting the rule or monarchy of God.[20] Throughout Paracelsus contrasted his active empirical approach to knowledge with the sterile authoritarianism of his opponents. His discourse is peppered with terminology signifying his faith in proof by 'experiment', for which he favoured analogy with the proving work undertaken by metalworkers. His terminology – Experienz, Experiment, Erfahrung etc. – was to dominate the experimental philosophy of the seventeenth century, and there is a substantial degree of overlap between the epistemology of Paracelsus and the Baconians. However the underlying science to which experiment contributed was viewed very differently. 'Science' was not merely the explanatory model built up by the observer on the basis of his observations, it was also in the opinion of Paracelsus a possession of the system under investigation. Science for instance was the property which enabled all things to retain their type.[21] And since the terrestrial being was in concordance with the heavens and also subject to emanations from celestial bodies, its 'science' could be regarded as an emanation from the stars.[22]

Despite his use of much of the vocabulary of modern experimental science, Paracelsus's view of science was firmly rooted in the tradition of spiritual magic. For Paracelsus the operative side of science involved bringing into action forces derived from the heavens. Mankind was in a unique position to exploit these forces by being situated at the 'boundary' or at the 'centre' between the heavens and the rest of creation; man was the 'medium', and operative science could be regarded as a form of magic. Only mankind was granted the capacity to unleash the virtues hidden in stones, plants, words and characters. The astronomer could be said to draw powers from the firmament into the individual.[23] At one level scientists would be involved in chemical manipulations, separating out the active principles of drugs, thought to be the equivalent of the pure essence derived from the stars; at another they would be counteracting with magical formulae, damage done by evil incantations. The model for this impressive command over nature was the *magus* of the scriptures, especially as exemplified by Moses, Solomon or the three Kings of the East, an image which the renaissance magicians were accustomed to conflate with its kinsman, the *magus* figure of hermeticism.[24]

Although hermetic elements inevitably impinged on Paracelsus's rendering of magic, this aspect of his worldview retained its fundamentally scriptural centre of gravity, and it was firmly related to his particular Christian social ethic. The magus only expressed natural powers by virtue of his status as a believer; the saint and the magus were really two sides of the same coin.[25] Paracelsus firmly believed that the essential capacities of the biblical magus were within reach of the renewed Christian of the scientific age. Not through books or secular learning, but only through the true faith could the powers of the magus be derived from the stars. A more hermetic view of the magus ideal of Paracelsus derives from the corpus of doubtful or spurious writings attributed to Paracelsus, and to the works of the early Paracelsians, sources which have deeply influenced historical accounts of Paracelsus himself and which prove that the Paracelsian movement was swept up in the hermetic tide which engulfed Europe in the late sixteenth century.

The Paracelsus idea of magic extends across a broad spectrum lying between traditional magic and experimental science. For the most part, at least in the genuine writings, the emphasis was firmly towards the latter. The intervention of the magus in nature was seen to be successful by virtue of his knowledge of natural processes, skill in manipulation, and direction of the forces inherent in nature, rather than by the employment of intelligences, or miraculous powers.[26] Thus, for the most part Paracelsus was an advocate and practitioner of natural magic, and much of what constituted natural magic for Paracelsus represented a fund of sound observations of a kind prerequisite for work in the experimental sciences developed in the course of the ensuing century. Much of what was rejected later, was also rejected by Paracelsus as credulous vanity.[27] He fully appreciated that the repute of legitimate magic was placed at risk by foolish or unscrupulous exploitation of ceremonies, conjurations, blessings, and curses.[28] There remained a penumbra having less certain status: the doctrine of signatures, physiognomy, and chiromancy persisted and seemed to be eminently reasonable areas for scientific speculation; hieroglyphs, characters, and emblems lost none of their effectiveness as a means of conveying and organizing information, and they continued to be regarded as a vehicle for the transmission of arcane truths from the ancient to the modern world.

Although expressed in his own characteristic language the idea of natural magic developed by Paracelsus coincided in major respects with the natural magic of the Neoplatonists. A sequence of authors from Ficino onwards, and including Pico della Mirandola, Trithemius, and Agrippa, placed magic at the heart of their system of ideas. Like Paracelsus they distinguished natural from demonic magic, emphasized the dependence of physical change on the earth, on forces derived from the heavens. They also believed that the understanding of these natural forces could be turned to operative effect, opening up for man the possibility of achieving by natural means what had hitherto been regarded as miraculous, that is occasioned by good or evil intelligences. All of this was to be attained by the skilful assistance, imitation, or direction of nature, an approach echoed by Bacon in the opening words of *Novum Organum* where mankind was heralded as 'the servant and interpreter of Nature'.

Natural magic became the vehicle for the projection of the term magic into the normal vocabulary of the sciences, so bringing about connotations of the transcendental potentialities of science in both its pure and applied forms. Ficino had firmly distinguished between the magus and the sorcerer, the magus being 'a contemplator of heavenly and divine science, a studious observer and expositor of divine things, a figure respected in the gospels, not signifying a witch or conjurer, but a wise man and priest'. Similarly Trithemius emphasized that his own practice of magic had nothing to do with the popular tradition, being based on the sophisticated knowledge of mathematics and concerned with the analysis of mathematical harmonies within nature. This 'natural magic' was pure, solid, and permissible, in contradistinction to the worthless magical cults of the illiterate. As Pico declared: 'Magic is the sum of natural wisdom, and the practical part of natural science, based on exact and absolute understanding of all natural things'. According to Pico, by the employment of acute observation rather than demons, the forces of the celestial world might be

brought to bear on the terrestrial world in order to perform natural works
rather than to seek miracles.[29] Agrippa affirmed that

> Magic comprises the most profound contemplation of the most secret
> things, their nature, power, quality, substance, and virtues, as well as
> the knowledge of their whole nature. It instructs us concerning the dif-
> ferences and similarities among things, from whence it generates its
> marvellous effects, by uniting the virtues of things by the application of
> one to another, joining and knitting together appropriate inferior sub-
> jects to the powers and virtues of superior bodies.[30]

The idea that the essence of magic was the application of 'agents to
patients' or 'actives to passives' became the hallmark of definitions of
natural magic from Roger Bacon to Francis Bacon. At one extreme this
idea involved an experimental approach to nature; at the other it implied
that the full operational utility of natural magic entailed the magi immers-
ing themselves in the harmonies of nature.

Agrippa complained that because the natural magicians were capable of performing operations that were 'above human reason', or 'before
the time ordained by Nature', they were thought by the uninformed to
aspire to perform miracles, and hence to be in league with the Devil. This
much was suspected of Agrippa, and the supposition that mathematicians
and natural magicians were merely learned conjurers persisted and was
used to stir up enmity against them. Conrad Gesner acknowledged that
Paracelsus was a clever physician, but warned that he was also a magician
who was guilty of consort with demons. This charge is more understand-
able in the case of those natural magicians hypnotized by the possibility of
individually attaining universal wisdom, a direction taken by Guillaume
Postel, Giordano Bruno or, in his later career, by John Dee. This mentality was responsible for generating such esoteric fantasies as the Rosicrucian brotherhood. By contrast Paracelsus had placed emphasis on the
operative aspect of natural magic, and he anticipated that the growth of
knowledge and amelioration of social conditions would be consequent
upon a massive collaborative effort of the kind exemplified by the division
of labour among craftsmen. This tendency towards the democratisation
of magic found its classic expression in such figures as della Porta, Bacon,
and Samuel Hartlib. At the social level this attitude towards natural
magic was averse to the exclusivism of secret brotherhoods of illuminati,
pointing instead in the direction of coordinated effort involving all classes
of operator, and the free exchange of information.

It was entirely consistent with the mentality of the Paracelsian type of
natural magic that its practitioners should recognize the advantages of
coordinated effort in the scientific field, and also apply their insights to
planning in the wider social and political spheres. The entire history of

natural magic is closely tied up with a profusion of schemes for academies and specialized societies as well as broader social and utopian proposals. Significantly enough, the first of the projected scientific societies to struggle into life seems to have been the Accademia dei Segreti (c. 1560) of Naples established at the house of Giambattista della Porta, whose *Magia naturalis* (1558) is regarded as the classic expression of the ethos of natural magic.[31] Thereafter numerous brotherhoods, academies and societies expressing scientific aims made a short-lived appearance before the Royal Society (1660) and the Académie des Sciences (1666) consolidated their position as permanent scientific societies.[32] Natural magic in one form or another was firmly linked to the history of organized science, and the prevalent attitude towards natural magic was reflected in the ethical standpoint of each particular organizational effort.

The above demarcation of two traditions of natural magic reflects a genuine polarization of attitudes which was recognized and debated at the time, and was crucial to the choice of ethical and practical alternatives within science. This division between the exoteric and esoteric expressions of natural magic, offered here as a useful working hypothesis, is not intended as an inflexible instrument for coercing all individuals into two rigidly defined camps. Nevertheless, reference to such a distinction might help to counteract the recent tendency to overlook the existence of tensions between the various social expressions of natural magic, in the interests of exaggerating the internal coherence of hermeticism and overdrawing the significance of such artificially propagated exotica as Rosicrucianism. Both constructions of natural magic contributed towards heightening expectations of science and they gave greater reality to the ideal of cultural renewal. Natural magic joined the various intellectual forces mobilized to create confidence in some kind of *renovatio mundi* in the wake of the destabilization of the old order of Europe.

Guillaume Postel was representative of a new breed of philosopher-prophets who captured the attention of the courts of Europe with their predictions of universal monarchy, universal wisdom and the brotherhood of mankind. Postel believed that the great drama of history was working itself out towards the *restitutio omnium* of the Great Sabbath Age. The signs of the unfolding of the providential plan were clear for all to see: humanist scholarship, and all secular and divine learning had made more progress in the last fifty years than in the previous thousand; the power and doctrine of former ages had been confronted by the authority of true reason. The pace of change was increasing: witness the recent voyages to the new world, and the dissemination of the arts of artillery and printing. Such things were contributing to the power and wisdom of the Christian peoples. Postel also realized that these changes were instrumental in giving all men the opportunity to contribute to the renovation of things, and hence to appreciate the truths of the new faith which he was preaching.[33]

More calmly rational than Postel, but conveying a very similar impression, were the prophecies of Tycho Brahe, supported in his case by astronomical evidence. As mentioned above Brahe confidently believed that Europe was standing at the dawn of a blessed age, when all peoples would be united in peace and concord. Kepler and Johann Valentin Andreae drew back from dogmatic prophecies and both were alarmed by the appeal exercised by the Rosicrucian myth. The great use of Paracelsus by the hermeticists tended to weaken his appeal for Andreae, who attacked the followers of Paracelsus, Schwenckfeld, and Weigel for believing that they were destined to accomplish universal reforms. Nevertheless sceptics like Kepler and Andreae maintained a sense of the forward rush of learning, and some confidence in universal wisdom and a utopian future, albeit in the context of a spiritual rather than a spatial or chronological construct.[34]

The degree to which magical and prophetic factors played a part in galvanizing the scientific movement of the seventeenth century has perhaps been underestimated in standard accounts of the Scientific Revolution. From their different corners of Europe, and almost simultaneously, Campanella, Andreae and Bacon recapitulated elements from Postel's interpretation of history, and each utilized a utopia to express their aspirations for the science of the future. For the most part they relied on natural magic to provide the sources of social amelioration, a connection emphasized by Bacon's inclusion of the plan for Solomon's House, an ideal scientific institution, in his *New Atlantis*, and also by the publication of *New Atlantis* in tandem with his *Sylva Sylvarum*, a work closely modelled upon della Porta's *Magia naturalis*. Nor was the prophetic element missing from the programmes for the new sciences. Campanella was still obsessed by the Joachimite idea of universal monarchy. Bacon presented his system as the means for the return of the dominion of man over nature, and his title pages appropriately related this theme to the prophecies of Daniel.[35] Alsted's *Encyclopaedia* and related writings, an important source of inspiration for the young Leibniz, were bound up with an elaborate millennial scheme. The pansophic enterprise of Alsted's younger associate Comenius operated within the same universalist context (see illustrations 7 and 15, pp.35 and 70).

One of Bacon's major goals and accomplishments was the emancipation of natural magic. Despite rhetoric to the contrary he was not able to disentangle himself from the metaphysical suppositions of many of the natural magicians and alchemists falling under his censure, but his methodology placed new emphasis on systematic and exhaustive enquiry, rather than depending on random collection of novelties. By this systematization of effort he believed that the balance could be shifted from admiration and novelty to utility and fruit.[36] He opened up prospects of restoring magic to its ancient place of dignity, and to the level of wisdom and knowledge achieved by the Persian *magi*, the three kings of the orient who came to worship at the birth of Christ. These ancients he believed were properly called *magi*, and the new system should aspire to their ends, the knowledge of hidden causes, the production of admirable works, and the artificial production of *magnalia* of nature.[37] *Sylva Sylvarum* was presented not as merely another miscellany of natural magic but as an adjunct to the specimen natural histories relating to nature and trades which formed the central preoccupation of Bacon's last years. *Sylva Sylvarum* in many respects became the most popular of Bacon's scientific and philosophical writings.

It is arguable that Bacon's programme for the reform of natural magic provided the dominant guiding principle for organized scientific activity in England for the rest of the seventeenth century. However, Baconian *natural history*, like its forerunner *natural magic*, was no static concept. The intention of contributing towards the Baconian scheme expressed by generations of experimental philosophers should not disguise significant shifts of emphasis, which in turn may be associated with the major ideological tensions experienced during the crisis-troubled century.

The first energetic pursuit of Baconian natural history on a systematic scale was the work of the social reformers of the Puritan Revolution.[38] Their activity was coordinated by Samuel Hartlib and much of it occurred under the aegis of his semi-official Office of Address. Natural history was adopted as the form of science most likely to lead to economic development and the solution of pressing problems of poverty. Consequently emphasis was firmly placed on the natural history of trade. Success on this front was seen as an asset to the survival and credibility of the Republic. The urgency of the economic and social problems of newly subjugated Ireland resulted in a concentration of effort there, one of the major outcomes being *Irelands Natural History* (1652), subsequently regarded as a pioneering attempt at a regional economic geography. The extension of this latter project involved, seemingly for the first time, the use of the questionnaire method of collecting scientific information. Histories of trade, framed with respect to various branches of the mechanical arts and agriculture, were the staples of this unglamorous form of scientific activity undertaken by Hartlib's team of forgotten followers. But it is also evident that this mission inspired the scientific enthusiasm of Boyle and Petty at the outset of their careers. Through them and Henry Oldenburg much of the spirit of this practical endeavour was carried over into the early Royal Society.

Baconian histories of trade now became the work of numerous committees of the great society. There was no sense at the time that the utilitarian aspect of science was any less prestigious, or of any lower priority than the better-known experimental case studies not obviously related to practical affairs.[39] In the *History of the Royal Society* drawn up in the Society's defence almost immediately after its foundation, histories of trade constituted a major propaganda weapon, underlining the value of the Society in the service of the Restoration state. Indeed the author of the *History* went so far as regarding the Royal Society as the 'Twin Sister' of the Royal Company of Adventurers Trading into Africa. The two bodies were founded simultaneously, contained an overlapping membership, and were the product of a similar ethos. Every effort was made to identify the Royal Society with the nation's economic interests, defence and imperial aspirations. John Evelyn's *Sylva*, an ostentatious specimen natural history contributing towards the work of the Royal Society's premier Georgical Committee, was dedicated to the Commissioners of the Navy, and Dryden's *Annus Mirabilis* alluded to the Royal Society in its digression on navigation.[40] Owing to the single-minded dedication of Henry Oldenburg, natural histories were propagated as a world-wide mission, questionnaires being issued to travellers, with a view to building up a data-gathering process extending beyond Europe to the British Colonies and into all spheres of trading influence.

It is well known that natural histories, along with other attempts at collaborative research, generated little in the way of finished work. Nevertheless, out of the patchwork of effort, certain local enthusiasts pushed their work towards conclusion, the most notable success being the series of county natural histories, beginning with Robert Plot's *Natural History of Oxfordshire* (1677) and *Natural History of Staffordshire* (1686). Plot became Secretary to the Royal Society and edited the *Philosophical Transactions* for a short time, as well as being the leading light of the Oxford Philosophical Society. By the end of the century some dozen county natural histories had been produced, mainly by fellows of the Royal Society, and others were projected.[41] While swearing fidelity to Bacon's ideal of natural history, these works departed widely from his scientific intentions. Plot stressed that his history aimed to explore the 'hidden Treasures of our Land' and assist the conquering of nature.[42] Indeed his own work contained useful material concerning certain trades, but in the main the strength of these books lay in their accounts of antiquities and miscellaneous rarities of natural history. They were more relevant to the museum of dead objects which Ashmole founded and of which Plot was curator, than to the world of experimental science in either its pure or applied forms. These natural histories owed more to Camden than to Bacon; they were produced under the patronage of aristocrats and they had become an adjunct to aristocratic taste. The histories suffered from the same disease which was leading to the fatal impairment of the Royal Society.

The county natural histories issued by fellows of the Royal Society draw attention to the presence within the Society of an influential group relatively out of touch and indeed out of sympathy with the mechanical philosophy in its various forms. Such figures as Aubrey, Ashmole, and Plot preserved to a remarkable degree the outlook of the natural magicians of the renaissance, and central to their scientific activities were alchemy and astrology. Ashmole's major literary exercise, his *Theatrum Chemicum Britannicum* (1652), aimed to bring back into scientific use a collection of largely inaccessible and almost forgotten medieval alchemical texts by British authors. Ashmole used this antiquarianism as the occasion for an elaborate defence of natural magic, arguing that its essential aim was the understanding of inner harmonies within the universe, with a view to obtaining insight into the workings of the universal spirit and the immortal seed of worldly things.[43] He agreed with Robert Gell, a mentor of the Cambridge Platonists, that this form of knowledge would reveal mysteries 'far greater than the naturall Philosophy now in use and reputation will reach unto'.[44] True wisdom would thus be learned through magic and the hermetic philosophers. Ashmole identified himself with Francis Bacon in defining the future goal of science as regaining the form of knowledge which had been the property of Adam before the Fall: that 'true and pure Knowledge of Nature (which is no other than what we call Natural Magick) in the highest degree of Perfection'.[45] Ashmole may have misjudged the future course of science, but there is no reason to believe that the attitude which he represented was obsolete within the educated classes. The importance attached to Ashmole's *Theatrum* is perhaps indicated by the fact that it was one of the few books in Newton's possession which he is known to have annotated heavily.[46] Newton also possessed a copy of Porta's *Magia naturalis*, the durability of ᵗʰᵉ reputation of which was manifest in the appearance of a substantial English edition in 1658 (reissued in 1669).

The tide of translations of Paracelsian and alchemical works which began in the 1650s continued uninterruptedly after the Restoration. Kindred works emanating from the continent such as the six-volume *Theatrum Chemicum* (1659–61) produced by Eberhard Zetzner (an extended edition of a compilation originally issued in 1602), or Knorr von Rosenroth's massive *Kabbala denudata* (1677–84) made a major cultural impact in England. The standard exposition of Paracelsus by Severinus achieved new prominence through the labours of William Davisson, a Scot who had become the first professor of chemistry at the Jardin du Roi in Paris and then physician to the King of Poland. Davisson's major work, appearing in 1660, was a massive commentary presented as an introduction to a new edition of Severinus's *Idea medicinae philosophicae*.[47]

The rise of Cartesianism and other convincing variants of the mechanical philosophy produced an inevitable backlash, partly aroused by fears of the materialistic dangers of science. Retreat into the categories of Neoplatonism and hermeticism promised protection against the divorce between God and His universe. The great reputation of the Cambridge Platonists, and the insatiable curiosity about hermeticism are indicative of the persistence of belief in the basic tenets of both spiritual and demonic magic. John Beale took comfort in the notion that God was 'substantially present in all the operations of all creatures', an idea which he believed could be traced back to those severe and deep 'gymnosophiaticall' philosophers, and which had been passed to the West by the druids and bards, before finally appearing in Paracelsus and his follower Croll, and in Robert Fludd; even Bacon 'had some delight in the best sense of the notion'.[48] Beale used the revival of natural magic against Fifth Monarchists, but he was in no doubt that prophecies of the golden age were on the eve of fulfilment. It was time for all believers to take advantage of the 'Light of all sorts' breaking out; they should 'unite together and joyne their strength and counsayles into the execution, performance, and practise of the best things and for the best ends' with the expectation of 'Man . . . by Light restor'd to the dominion over his own house, soe, by Magnalias that are brought to light, Hee is restored to a dominion over all the beasts of the field, over the birds of the ayre and over the fishes of the Sea'. In practical terms Beale anticipated that chemists would shortly master the art of transmutation, discover powerful medicines, and learn to prepare useful products from seemingly useless plants.[49]

The above comments outline the continuing symbiotic relationship between prophecy and natural magic. The rising capacities of natural magic vindicated prophecy, while prophecy guaranteed the successes of natural magic. Thus, the well-informed synoptic review of the progress of experimental science in Europe, produced by John Jonston, like Davisson a Scot settling in Poland, concluded with a defence of prophecy. It seemed to him that divines had at least emerged with sufficiently impressive analytical and linguistic skills to unlock the secrets of Daniel and the Apocalypse. Undeterred by disagreement on matters of detail between Mede and Alsted, the giants of the prophetic scene, Jonston believed that 'the Church should be in greater glory upon the earth yet, than ever it

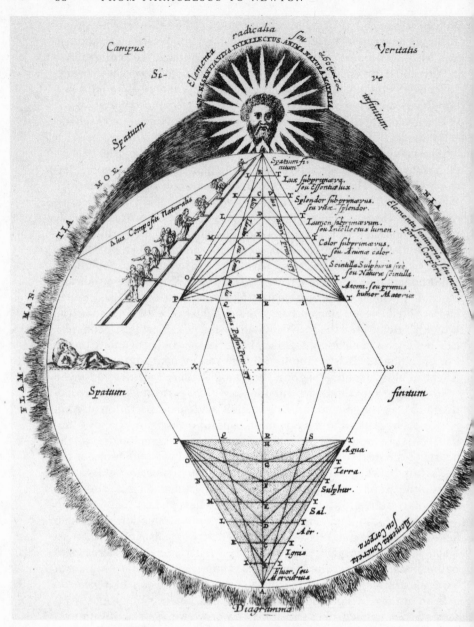

14.   From William Davisson, *Commentariorum . . . Ideam medicinae philosophicae.*

was before'.[50] Unwittingly, Jonston's translator connected the theme of his author's book with the iconography of Bacon's title pages and the title of the future apology for the Royal Society by Glanvill, in warning that 'they should not so much reflect on former times, as to forget that God had reserved something for them, if they would not be wanting in themselves. No *Hercules* Pillars are set up, with a *Non ultra* engraved upon them; but we are to make use of Charles the Fifth his Motto, and go on courageously with a *Plus ultra*'.[51]

With the Restoration in 1660 the above imagery was expropriated in its entirety, and adapted to a new purpose, the defence of the new royalist regime and all of its institutions. Beale wanted Boyle to take on the mantle of Bacon and undertake the completion of *Sylva Sylvarum*. Beale's other protégé John Evelyn, in the first public announcement of the existence of the Royal Society, identified the scientists with the *Annus mirabilis* of the new reign, and declared their intention to 'improve practical and Experimental knowledge, beyond all that has been hitherto attempted, for the Augmentation of Science and the universal good of Mankind'. Apologists for the Royal Society continued to press hard the identification of their effort with the general renewal they saw as occasioned by the Restoration.[52]

By this point it might be suspected that the imagery of the millennium was worn out and was being used as a cliché, rather than carrying conviction. But commentators such as Tuveson and especially Manuel and Jacob have demonstrated that this was not the case. As in earlier times the millenarian debate combined pessimism about the immediate future with expectations of providential deliverance in the longer term. Whether the New Heavens and New Earth would be realized before the Judgment and physical cataclysm was, as previously, a subject of fierce debate. The sense of imminent expectation was if anything increased by the hot pace of scientific progress in the later part of the century. Whiston regarded Newton's philosophy as an important component of the fulfilment of biblical prophecy, and a prelude to 'those happy times of the restitution of all things, which God has spoken of'.[53]

There was sharp disagreement among the cataclysmists concerning the degree to which the New Earth would replicate the physical conditions of the old. These speculations were handled with the confidence of a Postel or Bruno. With respect to the spiritual and social conditions envisaged for the millennial utopia, all of the conventional symbolism was brought into play. The new age would indeed be marked by 'UNIVERSAL PEACE AND UNITY'.[54] But on points of detail the image was more conventional and lacking in lustre. The future as presented by John Edwards bore striking resemblances to the present

> . . . those Happy Ages still abound with all things that conduce to the
> Welfare and Happiness of the *Body* as well as of the Soul, and con-
> sequently *Longevity* should be one of the Felicities of those times: And I
> doubt not but it will be procured by a perfect knowledge of the true
> Causes and Springs of Long Life, and of the more immediate Sources of
> Diseases. For *Natural Philosophy* . . . shall be then improved to the
> utmost, and a *Vertuoso* shall be no rarity . . . there will *a greater Number
> of Persons* upon the Earth in that Sabbathe Reign than there is now.
> This follows from what hath been said concerning that Universal Peace,
> that Extraordinary Measure of Bodily Health and Strength, that Dura-
> tion of Men's Lives, which shall be the Blessing of those Days.[55]

This was all summed up as the 'Evangelical Oeconomy'. It was something of an exaggeration to describe this state as a true realization of
'Dominion in the World' as understood by Paracelsus. It was more the
'Prosperous and flourishing State of the Church of Christ here on Earth'
in the Augustinian sense. The conservatism of this social image is in
strong contrast with the speculative energy devoted to the environmental
setting, so reversing the order of priorities in Paracelsus. Although called
a 'Sabbatical Reign', 'New Kingdom' or 'New Evangelical World', the
new order as conceived by Burnet, Edwards, Evelyn, or Whiston seemed
to consist of precisely the same economic and social order nourished by
the latitudinarians and consolidated by them after the Glorious Revolution. Fifth Monarchism was thus stripped of its magical and subversive
elements, and the residuum subsumed into the discipline of the church.

Persistence into the later seventeenth century of the sense of living in
the last age of the world, with the fear of divine judgment and the expectation that the efforts of the godly would be rewarded by the grant of earthly
paradise, supplied a continuing incentive to and a legitimation of engage-
ment in experimental science. This context helped to preserve the idea of
the scientist as a *magus* figure, even though natural magic had ceased to
be a completely dominant form of scientific expression. It can thus be
argued that Newton in particular saw himself as a *magus* figure intervening between God and His creation.[56]

It might be thought that natural magic acted as no more than a
generalized stimulus towards scientific activity, on the grounds that the
rambling edifice of Neoplatonic and hermetic metaphysics was gradually abandoned in the course of the seventeenth century in favour of the
streamlined categories of atomism and the mechanical philosophy. However, the case of Newton has already demonstrated that writings expressing the perspective of spiritual magic were not regarded merely as an
intellectual scrap heap reserved for antiquarians. The idea of harmony in
nature, parallelism between the macrocosm and microcosm, the perva-
siveness of forces akin to sympathy and antipathy, the application of

animistic explanations to directional processes, and reference to emanations and hierarchies that bridged the gulf between the material and non-
material world, remained viable explanatory options which were actively
drawn upon by forward-looking thinkers throughout the seventeenth
century. An essentially animistic view of creation was maintained by
Kepler and Gilbert, while Bacon also defies attempts to subject him to the
mechanical philosophy.[57] As Pagel has amply demonstrated Harvey and
his major disciple Glisson remained resolutely vitalist in their biological
philosophy.[58]

Even the French mechanical philosophers, the bastion of standard
interpretations of the rise of mechanism, on closer inspection are found to
be less rigidly consistent than hitherto we have been led to believe. In a
particularly important piece of self-conscious revisionism Bloch has not
only demonstrated close relations between Gassendi and such chemists as
Étienne de Clave, but has also established that the roots of Gassendi's key
unifying conception of *semina rerum generalia* derived directly from
Petrus Severinus, the codifier of Paracelsus.[59] Classical atomism was
adequate at the descriptive level, but it was found wanting when the need
arose to explain organized forms and vital processes. Bloch argues that
the single concept of 'seminal molecules', formed by the spontaneous
movement of atoms under the guiding force of semina, permitted Gassendi
to reconcile naturalism with creationism, materialism with vitalism,
animism with spiritualism, mechanism with final causes, and necessity
with Providence.[60] In other words the gulf between the atomist Gassendi
and the Platonism of Cudworth is considerably narrowed. We must now
re-examine the ontology and metaphysics of figures like Boyle to decide
the degree to which their Gassendian atomism also carried over the
Paracelsian notion of *semina rerum*. In view of a variety of links between
atomism and Paracelsianism a strong case could be made that Paracelsianism and atomism should not be regarded as mutually exclusive, but as
complementary modes of explanation.

The Cambridge Platonists carried the non-mechanistic view of nature
into the generation of Newton. Their conception of nature was not very
different from that expressed in the *Physica harmonica* (1612) or *Physicae
synopsis* (1628) of Alsted and Comenius respectively. More explicitly
than their Cambridge predecessors, Alsted and Comenius acknowledged
their debt to Paracelsus, Severinus, Sendivogius, Sennert, d'Espagnet,
and even more obscure sources touched by the magical tradition.[61] The
Cambridge authors rooted their ideas more directly in ancient theology,
but the aims of Alsted, Comenius and the Platonists coincided: the harmonization of knowledge derived from the Bible, Ancient Tradition and
Nature. This platform was by no means redundant by the time of Newton,

15.   Title page from Comenius, *Didactica Opera Omnia*.

whose deference to the scriptures and ancient tradition was quite equal to
that of the pansophists or Platonists. The relevance of the above programme to chemical theory and applied science is indicated by John
Webster's *Metallographia: or a history of Metals* (1671), arguably the
most effective work in its area produced by an English writer before 1700.
This book displays an all-round competence and solidity surprising to
those commentators who assess Webster solely on the basis of his polemical *Academiarum Examen* (1654). Yet, as in the earlier work, Webster
bases himself almost entirely on the literature within the natural magic
tradition.

This literature coincided exactly with the chemical works cited by Alsted
and Comenius, and the same works are represented almost in their entirety
in Newton's library. Newton's copy of Webster bears 'many signs of dog-
earing' as does the volume entitled *A New Light of Alchymie* (1650) containing translations of Sendivogius and Paracelsus.[62] The seriousness of
Newton's alchemical interest is now beyond doubt. That the alchemical
and Paracelsian literature contributed to Newton's thinking on the crucial
issue of active principles has been proposed as a working hypothesis.
Webster's book appeared at a strategically important moment in the formation of Newton's ideas on active principles and it contained much of direct and indirect relevance to this question. Active principles are likely to
become the substance of a debate as vigorous as any in the lively world of
Newtonian scholarship.[63] Whatever the outcome of this trial, the persistence into the later seventeenth century of the distinction between active
principles and passive matter is a reminder of the continuing reference to
categories bearing a generic resemblance to those implicit in the basic
definition of natural magic.

NOTES

1. P. Rossi, *Francesco Bacone: Dalla Magia alla Scienza* (Bari, 1957); W. Pagel,
   Paracelsus (Basel, 1958); F.A. Yates, *Giordano Bruno and the Hermetic
   Tradition* (London, 1964); *idem, The Rosicrucian Enlightenment* (London,
   1972); D.P. Walker, *Spiritual and Demonic Magic from Ficino to Campanella*
   (London, 1958).
      In the following pages the term 'natural magic' is used to denote that aspect
   of spiritual magic concerned with the interpretation and manipulation of
   physical phenomena.
2. *Auslegung des Cometen 1532*, PI, **9**, 414, 418; *De meteoris*, PI, **8**, 191.
3. *Sermo IV, De pseudodoctoribus*, cited from K. Goldammer (1952), Paracelsische Eschatologie II, *Nova Acta Paracelsica*, **6**, 68–102; pp.71–2, 96.
4. *Astronomia Magna*, PI, **12**, 320–32.
5. *Liber artis praesagis*, PI, **14**, 153.

6. *De secretis secretorum zu Matth. 24, 6,* cited from Goldammer, Paracelsische, Eschatologie, pp.72, 96.

7. *Labyrinthus medicorum errantium*, PI, **11**, 208–12.

8. *De fundamento scientiarum sapientiaeque*, PI, **13**, 295–7.

9. *Das Buch der Erkanntnus*, ed. K. Goldammer (Berlin, 1964), pp.27–9; *Labyrinthus medicorum errantium*, PI, **11**, 171–4.

10. *Astronomia Magna*, PI, **12**, 64–5. See illustration 10 (p.50).

11. *Psalmen Kommentar*, PII, **4**, 211, 294–5.

12. *Septem Defensiones*, PI, **11**, 127–8. For an iconographic expression of this idea by Comenius and Fludd, see illustrations 12, 13 and 15 (pp.53, 54, 70).

13. *Astronomia Magna*, PI, **12**, 382–6; *Liber de inventione artium*, PI, **14**, 249–53.

14. *Septem Defensiones*, PI, **11**, 127–36.

15. *Die Prognostikation auf 24 zukünftige Jahre*, PI, **10**, 580–3.

16. *Psalmen Kommentar*, PII, **7**, 75–6, 97–9; *Liber artis praesagis*, PI, **14**, 18–19.

17. Weimann, *Eine neu aufgefundene Paracelsus-Handschrift*, p. 355.

18. *Septem Defensiones*, PI, **11**, 141–6. *Volumen Paramirum*, PI, **1**, 174, 185.

19. J.S. Belkin and E.R. Caley, *Eucharius Rösslin the Younger: on Minerals and Mineral Products* (Berlin and New York, 1978).

20. *Labyrinthus medicorum errantium*, PI, **11**, 171–4.

21. *Labyrinthus*, PI, **11**, 190–5.

22. *Ganze Astronomei*, PI, **10**, 654.

23. *Astronomia Magna*, PI, **12**, 122, 460–1.

24. *Astronomia Magna*, PI, **12**, 369–71. See also *Fragmentum astronomicum*, PI, **12**, 507.

25. *Astronomia Magna*, PI, **12**, 130.

26. *Grosse Wundarznei*, PI, **10**, 352.

27. *Liber de imaginibus*, PI, **13**, 363–7, 380–2.

28. *De occulta philosophia*, PI, **14**, 538–42.

29. Ficino, *Opera*, 2 vols (Basel, 1576), **1**, 573; Trithemius to Joachim of Brandenburg, *Epistolarum* (Cologne, 1567), pp.100–16; Pico, *Opera omnia*, 2 vols (Basel, 1557–73), **1**, 167, 169–70 (*Apologia*); 327–31 (*De hominis dignitate*).

30. Agrippa, *De occulta philosophia*, I, 2, in *Opera*, 2 vols (Leyden, n.d.), **1**, 2.

31. N. Badaloni, *Introduzione a G.B. Vico* (Milan, 1961), pp. 9–12, and *passim*.

32. M. Ornstein, *The Role of Scientific Societies in the Seventeenth Century* (Chicago, 1928); N. Eurich, *Science in Utopia* (Cambridge, Mass., 1967).

33. W.J. Bouwsma, *Concordia Mundi: The Career of G. Postel* (Cambridge, Mass., 1957), p.271.

34. Andreae to S. Gloner, 14 August 1634, J.W. Montgomery, *Cross and Crucible, J.V. Andreae (1586–1654)* (The Hague, 1973), p.198.

35. See illustration 11 (p.51). This title-page was adapted for the 1640 English translation of *De augmentis scientiarum*.

36. Bacon, *Novum Organum*, I, 85, in *Works*, ed. J. Spedding, R.L. Ellis and D.D. Heath, 14 vols (London, 1857–74), **1**, 191–3.

37. Bacon, *Novum Organum*, I, 5, *Works*, **1**, 157; *De augmentis scientiarum, Works*, **1**, 571–5; *Cogita et visa, Works*, **3**, 591–2; *Filum labyrinthi, Works*, **3**, 496–7.

38. Webster, *Great Instauration*, pp. 420–83.

39. M. Hunter, *Science and Society in Restoration England* (Cambridge, 1981), pp.87–112.

40. Thomas Sprat, *History of the Royal Society* (London, 1667), p.407; McKeon, *Politics and Poetry*, pp.110–17; Dryden, *Annus Mirabilis*, clv–clxvi.

41. Porter, *The Making of Geology*, pp.38–41.

42. Plot, *Staffordshire*, Introduction.

43. Ashmole, *Theatrum Chemicum*, p.443.

44. *Theatrum Chemicum*, p.444. Robert Gell, *A Sermon Touching God's Government of the World of Angels* (London, 1650).

45. *Theatrum Chemicum*, p.446.

46. Harrison, *Library of Newton*, pp.93–4.

47. *Library of Newton*, pp.171, 220, 249. Newton possessed an earlier work by Davisson: *ibid.*, p.130. See illustration 14 (p.66). B.P. Copenhaver (1980), Jewish theologies of space in the scientific revolution: Henry More, Joseph Raphson, Isaac Newton and their predecessors, *Annals of Science*, **37**, 489–548.

48. Beale to Hartlib, 28 January 1658/9, Hartlib Papers LII, a reply to queries from Boyle's sister Lady Ranelagh. See illustrations 12 and 13 (pp.53 and 54).

49. Beale to Hartlib, 22 March 1658/9, Hartlib Papers LI. See illustration 9 (p.39) for the emblem of Comenius, originally produced for his *Via lucis*.

50. Jonston, *A History of the Constancy of Nature* (London, 1657), p.170. Original edition 1632. Glanvill, *Plus Ultra: or, the Progress and Advancement of Knowledge since the Days of Aristotle* (London, 1668).

51. *Constancy of Nature*, Preface. See illustration 11 (p.51), ships breaking out beyond the Pillars of Hercules.

52. Evelyn, *A Panegyric to Charles II* (London, 1661), p.14. See also *Diary*, ed. E.S. de Beer, 6 vols (Oxford, 1955), **3**, 239, and Preface to *Sylva* (1664). R.H. [doubtfully Robert Hooke], *New Atlantis Continued* (London, 1660), in his dedication to Charles II as 'Glorious Restaurator' identified Charles with Solomon and Justinian.

53. Whiston, *Memoirs*, **1**, 34.

54. Edwards, *Compleat History of All Dispensations*, p.736.

55. *Compleat History*, pp.744–5.

56. F. Manuel, *Portrait of Isaac Newton* (Cambridge, Mass., 1968).

57. G. Rees (1980), Atomism and 'Subtlety' in Francis Bacon's Philosophy, *Annals of Science*, **37**, 549–72.

58. Pagel, *William Harvey's Biological Ideas* (Basel/New York, 1967).

59. Bloch, *La Philosophie de Gassendi*, pp.249, 259, 270, 446. See illustration 14 (p.66).

60. Bloch, *Gassendi*, pp.455–6. See illustration 14 (p.66).

61. J. Červenka, *Die Naturphilosophie des J.A. Comenius* (Prague, 1970). See illustration 15 (p.70).

62. Harrison, *Library of Newton*, pp.236,260.

63. The initial rounds of this debate are summed up in J.E. McGuire and P.M. Rattansi (1966), Newton and the 'Pipes of Pan', *Notes and Records of the Royal Society of London*, **21**, 108–43; B.J. Dobbs, *The Foundation of Newton's Alchemy* (Cambridge, 1975); K. Figala (1977), Newton as Alchemist, *History of Science*, **15**, 102–37; J.E. McGuire, Neoplatonism and Active Principles: Newton and the *Corpus Hermeticum*, in R.S. Westman and J.E. McGuire, *Hermeticism and the Scientific Revolution* (Los Angeles, 1977); R.S. Westfall, *Never at Rest*, pp.286–308 and *passim* – summarizing various of his earlier contributions.

4 DEMONIC MAGIC

If there is room for doubt whether spiritual magic was rendered obsolete by the rise of experimental science, there would seem to be far less doubt concerning the survival of demonic magic. In a world system which with increasing effect explained physical change in mechanical terms, made minimal concessions to final causes, and which recognized the force of the Cartesian position concerning the dualism of spirit and matter, there would seem to be no occasion for invoking the active intervention of personalized demons in the affairs of the universe and mankind.

The mechanical philosopher's exclusion of demons from the field of the sciences might almost seem like an unnecessary exercise since personalized demons, by the seventeenth century, had apparently lost their place in scientific explanation. Of wider historical importance was the fact that the mechanical philosophy undermined the rationale for witchcraft, thereby dealing the final blow to a belief which had proved tenacious even among the educated classes, and which had ensured the survival of witchcraft prosecutions on an extensive scale, well into the seventeenth century. If valid this claim would constitute one of the major contributions of the Scientific Revolution towards the modernization of belief systems. Once freed from the ancient shackles of demonology, the way was clear for the more scientific investigation of many of the phenomena associated with witchcraft, and for the more humane and medical treatment of the persons affected. The witch-crazed world of Paracelsus seems to be light-years away from the enlightened scepticism of the age of Newton.

There can be no doubt concerning the strength of belief in demonic magic in European thought on the eve of the Scientific Revolution. Faced with coming to terms with the relics of pagan religious beliefs, the Christian church had increasingly identified the 'demons' of pagan religion and folk belief with fallen angels, and hence came to regard them as the agents of the Devil. The widespread and persistent belief in demons among the population was used to buttress the Christian idea that Satan and his followers were actively at work in the world seeking the destruction of souls (see illustration 16, p.76). Christian demonology firmly consigned minor demons, such as the fairies and nymphs of popular belief, into the class of evil spirits. Medieval theologians built upon the ideas of Augustine to elevate the role played by demons in the spread of heresy. The threat

16. *Ars Moriendi* [Lyon, *c.*1490] after the Master ES.

offered by Satan seemed to be growing rather than receding. Magical operations, regardless of their intentions, were regarded as mediated by demons; accordingly all magic risked becoming identified with witchcraft. By a further escalation, magic was assumed to require a positive pact with the demons. Hence all involvement with magic or acceptance of traditional beliefs concerning local spirit beings courted the charge of witchcraft.[1]

Much of the popular lore relating to demons was recited and condemned in the *Canon Episcopi*, a ninth- and tenth-century compendium which was treated with unmerited veneration before the seventeenth century, owing to confusion concerning its origin and status. Regardless of its provenance the *Canon Episcopi* met the needs of authority, and it provides valuable insight into church policy with respect to witchcraft and demonology before *Malleus Maleficarum*. *Episcopi* warned of the endemic belief in 'illusions and phantasms of demons', especially among women. Such beliefs were closely identified with incantations to provoke passions, or to harm property or persons. Participation or belief in such practices of necessity involved subservience to the demonic horde and their master. Especially dangerous pollution was thought to be inherent in beliefs and practices concerning incubi and succubi, and related sexual fantasies. *Episcopi* did not exempt from criticism seemingly innocent beliefs and customs concerning spirits, fairies, or little men, whose goodwill was courted in order to secure good fortune at work and protection of the home.[2]

The *Canon Episcopi* provided guidelines for action against witchcraft in the late medieval period, general metaphysical justification being supplied on the basis of biblical and Neoplatonic demonology in conjunction with Aristotelian physics. Many rival classifications of demons were utilized as an aid to propaganda, all serving to emphasize the ubiquity of the threat offered by the forces of evil. One popular classification emanated from the Byzantine polymath, Michael Psellus. His scheme outlined the characteristics of six classes of malicious demon; more widely preferred was a nine-fold classification. Such classifications were often cited in conjunction with others relating to the divisions of Aristotelian cosmology. Combinations of these schemes were repeated with minor variations by numerous authorities throughout the renaissance, in detail by such compilers as Georg Pictorius and Jean Bodin, or more superficially by Sebastian Munster and Olaus Magnus. Their point of view was aptly summarized by Bodin: 'Car les Faunes, Satyres, Sylvains, ne sont rien autre chose, que les Daemons, et malins esprits'.[3]

In the face of the above formulations, advocates of Neoplatonism and hermeticism needed to tread warily in order to avoid suspicion of heresy.

Intrinsic and fundamental to their cosmology was the idea of a hierarchy of intelligences pervading the sublunary world, as a manifestation of the universal cosmic spirit. These intelligences were readily construed as demons, with whom the philosophers might be supposed to consort. Some effort was made by Neoplatonists to minimize the part played by personalized spirits in their system, placing their emphasis rather on impersonal spiritual agencies, in order to avoid the accusation of polytheism and involvement in demonic magic. Nevertheless personalized demons tended to intrude into these systems, and at least in principle it was accepted that *intelligentiae separatae* represented a hierarchy paralleling the hierarchy of angels. Such demons inhabiting the earthly regions were thought to possess souls and aetheric or aerial bodies, and to exist as good or bad forms, only the latter being capable of disturbing man's imagination and spirits, and ultimately threatening his soul. The demons inhabiting the four elements in the terrestrial sphere were the counterpart of hosts of demons inhabiting the celestial regions, so contributing to the divine plenum. The one or the other class of celestial demons was thought to be responsible for meteors, comets, and other supernatural effects in the air which were regarded as miraculous forebodings tending to occur at moments of crisis. The Neoplatonists not only adopted an animistic conception of planetary bodies, but also linked the planets and stars with divine intelligences.[4]

In the wake of *Malleus Maleficarum* commentators from all sections of the church redoubled their efforts to identify spirits as the agents of the Devil. Even Johannes Trithemius, notorious as a dabbler in magic, and alleged conjuror of evil spirits, came out with strongly worded statements reiterating the line of current demonologies, and expressing support for stamping out witchcraft and necromancy, both of which were regarded as indicative of the prevalence in the population of active consort with evil spirits. Trithemius added lurid detail to the standard classification of the six types of elemental spirit, emphasizing the particular malignities of each genus of demon. Of all types, the subterranean 'devils' were regarded as the worst and most dangerous. All manner of mining accidents were blamed on these devils. They were also credited with enticing simple people into their lairs and impressing these folk with their magical tricks, and with stealing and amassing treasure. Trithemius believed firmly that subterranean devils could take on anthropomorphic characteristics.[5] Such views indicate the degree to which traditional demonology was becoming infused with elements from local folk belief.

Notwithstanding pressures to conform with the dominant line concerning witchcraft and demonology, humanistic theologians and natural philosophers of a variety of persuasions kept alive the debate, prevented the consolidation of opinion, and questioned many of the prevailing attitudes. From the Aristotelian camp Pomponazzi eliminated any idea of the participation of demons or angels in nature, all physical change being ascribed to physical causes as conceived within the Aristotelian framework. Neoplatonists such as Champier and Agrippa accepted that demons actively tormented mankind, and that these demons could be conjured up and appear to man in a variety of forms such as monsters, incubi or succubi, or giants. Involvement in occult arts associated with evil spirits was seen as offering a major threat to the Christian faith. Nevertheless it was also urged that much of what was claimed by conjurers and necromancers was merely sleight of hand, or alternatively the operation of the deluded imagination. Champier was satisfied that stories of witches flying or attending sabbaths were products of the imagination of the witch, when worked upon by the malign demon. In addition to presenting the orthodox opinion Champier cited the Arabic medical view that incubus could be regarded as a pathological condition.[6] Agrippa made a dramatic intervention in a witchcraft trial in order to demonstrate the extent of malpractice within the Inquisition. He remained unrepentant, reserving some of his fiercest polemic for the Inquisition in *De vanitate scientiarum*, and even composing a separate tract against the inquisitors, a work which was circulated in manuscript form, and all copies of which seem to have been destroyed.[7]

A further point of divergence between Neoplatonists and their critics related to the status of beneficent demons. Champier and Agrippa accepted that malignant and beneficent demons were involved in a struggle for the mind of man, with the former being placed at an advantage because they were more numerous and persistent. But Agrippa was reluctant to follow the establishment by identifying the spirits of popular lore as agents of the devil, being sympathetic to the popular belief that beneficent spirits could be cultivated with a view both to overcoming their evil counterparts, and achieving material advantages through their good offices. It was accepted that beneficent spirits possessed human propensities, enjoyed human company, and liked to live among human beings and their domestic animals. These spirits were particularly attracted to children, women and poor people. This disinclination to dwell on the intrinsic evil nature of demons was consonant with the experience of Georg Agricola, the famous writer on mining and metallurgy. Undoubtedly drawing upon the lore prevailing among miners, Agricola acknowledged that malicious demons sometimes made mines unworkable; but in general they were good omens. In describing demons he created for the first time our portrait of the archetypal dwarf. These dwarfs were portrayed as good-natured little men, working alongside the miners, with whom they lived in mutual accord.[8]

Theologians were already at the time of Paracelsus adding their notes of reservation to the extreme witchcraft position. It was urged that by attributing independent powers over nature to witches or demons, the witch hunters were tending to detract from the power of Providence. It was therefore better to regard catastrophes of the type attributed to witches as chastisement, warning, and testing by God, thereby preserving the image of the absolute authority of God in the universe. Witches were merely deluded into believing that they were the cause of storms, crop failures, and harm to persons and domesticated animals. The guilt of witches was thus seen as lying more in falling into temptation, than in accomplishment of any physical harm.[9]

Notwithstanding the above reservations, the belief that the Devil was granted powers to wreak physical effects and that this power was exercized by human beings for malicious ends by virtue of some kind of pact with the Devil, was undoubtedly endemic at the time of Paracelsus. This was the intellectual basis upon which the notorious witch trials spread epidemically throughout Europe. Nevertheless, as indicated above, from the outset there was no complete consensus of opinion concerning witchcraft, even within official circles, and intellectuals expressed widely divergent views, extending even to complete scepticism. The widening of the sphere of operation of natural magic itself led to the erosion of the explanatory role of demonic magic, with the result that the Neoplatonist and hermeticist was in possession of a weapon which could be turned against witchcraft beliefs.

Paracelsus is an enigmatic witness on the question of witchcraft and demonic magic. His writings have been plundered to present him as totally immersed in sorcery and witchcraft beliefs. Equally he has been presented as the first major modern medical thinker to break decisively with medieval demonology, and the first to investigate behavioural disorders with the eyes of a modern clinician. If stripped of their anachronistic elements both constructs are legitimate, and they are not entirely irreconcilable.[10] The worldview of Paracelsus saw no contradiction in amalgamating acute clinical observations with insights gained from popular belief. Unlike other Neoplatonists and hermeticists Paracelsus made little attempt to distance himself from the world of popular belief. He was averse to superstition, but superstition was not regarded as the monopoly of the lower orders. Paracelsus consciously aimed at a synthesis which would make the maximum use of knowledge gained by the light of nature. Hence it was necessary to avoid sorcery, ghosts, spirits, or any beliefs which would lead in the direction of the heretical sects. It was one of his maxims to 'keep sorcery out of medicine'.[11]

In view of the above comments, it seems something of a contradiction to the modern reader that Paracelsus went along with what was commonly believed about the Devil and his threats to mankind. The Devil and his legions were never far from the scene in the writings of Paracelsus. The hierarchy of good spirits in the universe was matched by a formidable army of evil spirits, sent by God to test the faithful.[12] The Devil was as watchful over a man, as a cat over a mouse.[13] For those found wanting evil spirits served as God's executioners or hangmen, primarily by providing the grounds for punishment in the next world.[14] Evil spirits were not limited to tempting mankind to moral failings. They had once been angels and had been gifted with angelic wisdom. God permitted them to retain this intrinsic ability, which was exploited by the evil spirits to procure great knowledge about the powers of nature, which they could then use to teach men to do harm. Their skills tended to transcend those of man by virtue of their long life and great mobility. Anyone in consort with evil spirits could mobilize this *magia infernalium* to unlock the secrets of nature.[15]

Despite recognizing the enticing qualities of evil spirits, however, Paracelsus placed strong limits on their power, primarily on the basis of the principle that evil spirits remained in a position of complete dependence on God. Without God's permission they were impotent; like constables they acted only in response to His magistracy. Paracelsus was also hesitant to ascribe to evil spirits direct powers of interference with terrestrial bodies. Occasionally, he wrote as if they were made to activate adverse natural processes such as storms at the direct behest of God, as punishments for human wickedness. More usually, their powers were used as a direct aid to witchcraft, for instance, by reinforcing the power of the imagination of the witch.[16] Most frequently Paracelsus limited them to teaching evil arts, and to infusing mankind with evil thoughts.[17]

The arts taught by evil spirits relied on the same physical principles as in natural magic, but the spirits facilitated more dramatic manifestations such as storms, or the dematerialization of objects for injection into the bodies of the victims of witchcraft.[18] Thus the storm caused by the witch was precisely the same as the tempest occurring naturally, but the evil spirit was used to sow the seeds, or catalyse the normal chemical and physical processes associated with tempests.[19] When it rained frogs, the frogs were not derived from the skies, but originated in the normal way on the earth, before being drawn by a magnetic power into the clouds, and returning to the earth in a storm.[20] But one of the most potent forces at the disposal of the witch for harming a victim was the power of imagination. This psychic force was regarded as a source of discomfort, sterility, disease, even epidemics, without involving the direct intervention of evil spirits.[21] This power was thought to be exercised in the customary way by the witch damaging the appropriate part of a wax or bread figurine.[22]

Contact with evil spirits was by means of ceremonial magic closely allied by Paracelsus to the ceremonial of the Popes or Pharaohs, who, he claimed, had raised spirits to the level of gods and become their servants rather than their masters.[23] All ceremonies, whatever their purpose, were suspect, intended either to defraud, or to make contact with evil spirits.[24] He regarded all ceremonies, conjurations, blessings or curses, burning of holy candles, ringing of bells, as perversions of magic by witches and sorcerers.[25] Such destructive magic was seen as a serious threat to the health of the individual and to the economic well-being of the community. The sorcerer and the witch were accordingly acknowledged to be the community's most dangerous enemies. While Paracelsus almost never mentioned countermanding action other than protection or cure, on one occasion he acknowledged that the sorcerer deserved to be executed by fire.[26]

Paracelsus was not unduly perturbed by witchcraft in particular, which he believed could be answered by protective magic, a view consistent with his thesis that the cure must be related to the aetiology of the condition.[27] Thus in this case the construction of a wax figurine by the witch needed to be answered by the destruction of a wax figurine by the magician. Equally, injections needed to be treated by appropriate sympathetic magic. Paracelsus realized that magical cures of this kind might be frowned upon by the medical establishment, but on these matters he believed that the lore of old wives, gypsies, black magicians, travellers, old peasants and similar simple people was more relevant than the teaching of the medical schools. However, magical cures needed to be used with care in order for the user not to slide into the use of illicit practices.[28]

The description of the witch by Paracelsus is a folklore classic. Besides being an adept in destructive magic, the witch was characterized by crooked appearance, secretive habits, anti-social behaviour, avoidance of marriage, and especially the ability to fly on a pitchfork to the sabbath held by witches and evil spirits. Paracelsus often alluded to the wild gatherings (*Wütenden Heer*) supposed to be held in the remote *Heuberg*.[29] There the witches would take part in ceremonies using such traditional ingredients as cat and wolf grease and asses' milk. They would indulge themselves with incubi and succubi, or with wandering night spirits, which would carry sperm between humans and impure animals such as goats, dogs, worms and toads, with the result that vile monsters could be generated from these illicit unions.[30] The Devil could of course transmute witches into such forms as dogs, cats or werewolves.[31]

Thus far there is little to separate Paracelsus from his more orthodox contemporaries in his assessment of witchcraft, except perhaps for his greater emphasis on the power of the imagination in the generation of disease and his more indirect attribution of malignant acts to evil spirits than was often the case. However, the differences in emphasis extended further in some important respects:

First, Paracelsus made remarkably little reference to witches engaging in pacts with evil spirits, usually a keynote in definitions of witchcraft. On one occasion he explicitly denied that such pacts or covenants were made by the Devil.[32] This omission is consistent with the view of Paracelsus that the witch was essentially a physical and personality type, whose character, like that of other types such as the deformed, disabled, thief or murderer, is determined at the moment of conception.[33] Thus the pact with the Devil was unnecessary to the witch type, and none other than this type was given the capacity to make such pacts. The set of dominant characteristics, or *Ascendent*, of the witch is inherited from the parents, and is thus a reflection of the hereditary line or *ens seminalis*. This hereditary constitution, rather than any tendency implanted by the stars at birth, was responsible for any expression of character. Contrary to general belief, it was asserted that 'the stars do not control anything in us, they mold nothing in us, they do not irradiate anything, they bias nothing; they are free by themselves and we are free by ourselves'.[34] The Neoplatonic view that births under Saturn inclined towards melancholy and hence witchcraft was not accepted by Paracelsus. The relevance of the stars to the understanding of health and disease lay in other directions, such as determination of the quality of the environment, and providing a model for the working of the microcosm. The only interference with the operation of the *ens seminalis* came through the working of the imagination of parents at the time of conception. This might lead to minor deformity, and an imagination distorted by immorality would, at an extreme, lead to the production of monsters, succubi or incubi.[35]

The *spiritus* or *Geist* of the child is dormant, and only slowly does it develop under the influence of the *Ascendent* – its master. In the case of the witch the *Ascendent* excites envy, hate and vindictiveness. These urges are developed in the course of dreams, which act as lessons in the illicit arts which when realized enable the witch to turn instincts into action. It is also the *Ascendent* which leads to the abnormal sexual behaviour of witches and to their sterility.[36]

Secondly, Paracelsus revised traditional demonology to reclassify as beneficent beings intelligences which were regarded by the church as malignant demons. It has been noted above that Agrippa and Agricola emphasized the beneficent nature of many of the spirits associated with home and work. Paracelsus went further and removed these beings altogether from the realm of the spirit world, regarding them as a special category of being, part human, part animal, and part spirit: they 'die with the beasts, walk with the spirits, eat and drink with men'. They were Sir Thomas Browne's 'non-Adamicall men, or middle natures betwixt men and spirits'.[37] These beings were not only quite distinct from demons, they were themselves likely to be possessed by evil spirits. On the basis of this reclassification it became legitimate for men and women to inter-marry with these creatures, with whom they were supposed to bear nor-mal offspring. Dwarfs, and their equivalents, were cast as models for social values, experts in the arts, and as incorruptible agents of virtue, sent by God to be imitated and granted by him powers of retributive jus-tice. These formidable but elusive beings took responsibility for much of what might hitherto have been investigated as witchcraft. Robin Hood legends performed a very similar function.

Thirdly, Paracelsus drastically extended the scope of naturalistic expla-nation for disease. Under the Paracelsian concept of witchcraft, the abnormal manifestations associated with this condition were confined to the narrow group displaying the complex syndrome for witchcraft. No single characteristic was sufficient for identifying the witch, only the whole ascendancy. Thus the very comprehensiveness of the Paracelsian description of the syndrome was a guarantee that most deviancy would fall short of his criteria. Hence a vacuum was created, and Paracelsus came forward with convincing alternative explanations for what might commonly have fallen by default into the witchcraft category.

It has already been pointed out that much attributed by others to the action of evil spirits was recognized by Paracelsus as the effect of the direct influence of the imagination of one person on another. Other com-mon behavioural disorders such as hysteric symptoms and delusions dis-played by pregnant women, he regarded as being induced by their condi-tion, so anticipating the argument associated with Johann Weyer that such women could not be regarded as witches.[38] Epilepsy, mental defi-ciency and various behavioural disorders were classified into a variety of compartments, each provided with a separate naturalistic explanation, and in only residual categories was the possibility of demonic possession admitted. Another eliminating principle adopted by Paracelsus stated that the Devil was impotent to enter bodies not ruled entirely by reason.[39] Taking a further step away from his contemporaries Paracelsus recog-nized that the idiot's total deprivation of animal reason provided com-plete protection from the depredations of sin, thereby elevating him in the eyes of God. The idiot was therefore not to be scorned, or persecuted as if possessed, but like the little people should be cherished as a model for teaching spiritual lessons to the community.

By contrast with his prophetic writings the tracts by Paracelsus touching on witchcraft were published only posthumously, and generally after a delay of more than twenty-five years. Nevertheless his scattered comments on demonic magic and witchcraft attracted widespread interest both before and after the publication of the genuine writings, as indicated by attention to these subjects in some of the best known of the extensive body of works of doubtful authenticity. Writings from this latter category, such as *De occulta philosophia,* became among the most widely published and translated of the Paracelsian writings. Importantly from a practical point of view, the ideas of Paracelsus were taken into acount by influential moderates on the question of witchcraft, such as the Lutheran theologian Jacob Heerbrand, whereas hardliners like Thomas Erastus needed to devote great energy to the refutation of the Paracelsian position. Tycho Brahe, a strong partisan of the Paracelsian party, slyly remarked that if the attacks of Erastus upon astrology and Paracelsian medicine rested on no better grounds than the defence of the Aristotelian theory of comets, neither the astrologers nor the Paracelsians had anything to fear from him.[40]

In the longer term the greater influence on the question of witchcraft was exercised by Johann Weyer, the disciple of Agrippa, whose ideas were expressed in a single systematic treatise, rather than being diffused through a vast corpus of more general medical writings, as in the case of Paracelsus.

It is very difficult to sustain the deeply held view that Weyer's *De praestigiis daemonum* (1563) is one of the great modern medical classics, or that its author was a neglected if not persecuted figure of the proto-enlightenment.[41] Too much attention has been paid to the violent denunciation of Weyer by Bodin. Weyer's book was not thereby discredited; it attracted continuous comment, much of it favourable.[42] During the century after its first appearance Weyer's work was expanded, republished and translated into French and German, usually being cited as just one example among a not-inconsiderable body of literature critical of some aspect of witchcraft beliefs. Contemporaries formed a correct estimate of the stature of Weyer. The great history of medicine by Sprengel raised Weyer to an artificial eminence as a rationalist benefactor of the human race, and only recently has it become possible to risk a more critical approach to his work.[43]

Weyer summarized much previous adverse opinion concerning the treatment of old women accused of witchcraft. His major advance was to assert that these women were deluded and falsely accused. Weyer took advantage of invaluable supporting evidence on the hallucinogenic effects of narcotics deriving from the natural magicians Cardano and della Porta. Weyer was in certain respects more radical than Paracelsus, notably in his

unwillingness to concede the real existence of the syndrome of characteristics associated with witches, in particular with respect to women. The
whole of this bizarre lore was either dismissed as delusion or superstition,
or explained naturalistically.

But this was only part of the story. Weyer compensated for his position
on the witchcraft syndrome by conceding the ubiquity of the Devil in
nature, this influence extending to the widest range of physical operations, and posing a constant threat to the faith of believers. In essence, the
demonology of Weyer was quite as comprehensive and bizarre as that of
his supposedly more gullible contemporaries. He accepted that those suc-
cumbing to the temptations of demons deserved the harshest punishment, and his sensitivity to the threat of victimization of such exposed
groups as the mentally disadvantaged was by no means as apparent as in
the case of Paracelsus. Intrinsically Weyer's medical standpoint was that
of conservative humoral pathology, for the most part derived from
Arabic medical sources. His methods of therapy were equally conventional, and this brought him into sharp conflict with Paracelsianism,
which he recognized as a powerful force, even among educated physicians. He regarded Paracelsian medicine as an unwholesome mixture of
sorcery and dangerous cures, making far too many concessions to popular
beliefs and practices concerning magic.

Thus Weyer occupied an anomalous position, and found himself uncom-
fortably wedged between the warring camps of medicine: defending
Agrippa, but attacking Paracelsus; being attacked by Erastus, by whom
he was bracketed with Paracelsus. As with Paracelsus the complexities of
Weyer's position have tended to be lost sight of by modern commentators
who have only been concerned with his points of contact with modern
psychological medicine. More realistically, Weyer indicates the
emergence of a degree of scepticism concerning witchcraft accusations
even within the ranks of the conservative Galenic physicians.

Regardless of the question of the modernity of their positions, figures
like Agrippa, Paracelsus and Weyer indicate the openness of the sixteenth century debate on demonology and witchcraft. This critical position was not the dominant one within the ecclesiastical and civil establishment, but the intellectual following for the reformers was considerable.
Even in England Reginald Scot, otherwise known only as a pioneer writer
on the cultivation of hops, produced a major exposition of the case against
witchcraft, considerably in advance of Weyer in the radicalism of its position and the consistency of its argument. Keith Thomas recognizes Scot's
work as an expression of a 'continuing stream of scepticism throughout
the whole period of witchcraft prosecution in England'.[44] From the later
sixteenth century onwards in scientifically informed circles there was full

recognition of the viability of medical explanations of witchcraft phenomena. The celebrated puritan divine William Perkins needed to warn learned 'patrons of witches' that they were 'greatly deceived in fathering the practises of sorcery upon a melancholike humour'.[45] The medical sceptics who expressed themselves publicly ranged from the astrological physician John Harvey, the brother of Gabriel Harvey, to John Cotta, the humble practitioner from Northampton. The latter dwelt at length on the profusion of unsavoury practices and practitioners associated with magic, but he also called for the exercise of much greater critical discrimination in the case of witchcraft. Cotta said that he did not 'denie or defend divellish practises of men and women, but desire only to moderate the general madnesse of this age, which ascribeth unto witchcraft whatsoever falleth out unknowne or strange unto a vulgar sense'. He outlined numerous cases from his own experience in which the strangest behavioural abnormalities might be explained naturalistically, warning that it was unwise to accept witchcraft as the cause, even when willing confessions were forthcoming.[46]

The lack of consensus, even among the elite of the medical profession, is illustrated by one of the rare cases in which the College of Physicians of London was drafted in to testify in a witchcraft trial. The College in 1602 seems to have been divided concerning the case of an adolescent girl who was the alleged victim of witchcraft at the hands of an old charwoman. The most vehement and most actively publicized contribution to the debate came from the young physician Edward Jorden, who identified the girl's condition as hysteria, or in vernacular terms, suffocation of the mother. But the testimony of Jorden and his like-minded colleague John Argent (later dedicatee of Harvey's *De Motu Cordis*), failed to save the charwoman from being sentenced to imprisonment and the pillory. The physicians disagreeing with Jorden failed to detect conditions which might be unambiguously ascribed to witchcraft. Rather, being unable to explain or cure the disease naturalistically, they merely fell back on supernatural explanation by a process of elimination. At least four of the Fellows inclined to the witchcraft explanation vigorously propounded by Stephen Bredwell, a licentiate of the College.

This story gives very little assistance to any view which would ascribe to the medical elite strong support for the conclusions of the judge that 'the Land is full of Witches'.[47] Nevertheless this latter belief persisted and in the instability of the times found expression in panic. In 1647 James Howell gathered together evidence for witchcraft declaring that 'since the beginning of these unnatural wars there may be a cloud of witnesses produced for the proof of this black tenet'.[48] The Civil War by no means marked the end of witchcraft trials, but Britain was experiencing the last

epidemic of witchcraft executions. Gradually the waves of witch persecution subsided into perturbations of ever-decreasing extent, a transformation which among other things is thought to be indicative of a falling-off in
witchcraft beliefs among the educated classes.

At the popular level, there is no reason to suppose that there was a
decline of belief in such demonic tribes as the 'terrestrial devils', for
example 'lares, genii, fauns, satyrs, wood-nymphs, foliots, fairies, Robin
Goodfellows, trolli etc., which as they are most conversant with men, so
they do them most harm'.[49] For protection against such evils it was known
to be the habit of the people in every county to consort openly 'with white
witches whom the ignorant people dignifie no less than demigods, styling
them with the titles of wise or cunning men or women'.[50] These practices
were of considerable annoyance to the more orthodox medical practitioner, but popular attitudes persisted. Later in the seventeenth century
it was still a source of complaint that the 'common people, if they by
chance to have any sort of Epilepsie, Palsie, Convulsions, and the like, do
presently perswade themselves that they are bewitched, forespoken,
blasted, fairy-taken, or haunted with some evil spirit'. Nothing would
convince them otherwise. The wise sceptic should 'indulge that fancy, and
seem to concur in opinion with them, and hang any insignificant thing
about their necks, assuring them that it is a most efficacious and powerful
charm . . . and so you may cure them, as we have done in great numbers'.[51] Thus even the sceptic was obliged to use magical cures and treat
diseases as if they were caused by witchcraft, sorcery, or by some demonic
being.

Because the decline of witchcraft persecutions coincided exactly with
the rise of the new science, there is every inducement to assume causal
connections between the two trends. Nothing could seem more reasonable than the elimination of witchcraft beliefs in the wake of the mechanical philosophy which in either its Cartesian or Hobbesian form created a
new confidence in the ability of science to explain mental and physical
phenomena in terms of the laws of matter and motion. Such a worldview
would seem to eliminate any possibility of the role of intelligences,
whether good or evil, in the explanation of physical change.

It would furthermore be anticipated, and indeed has been loosely
assumed, that enlightenment on the question of witchcraft would filter
down from the scientific community, and that leadership on this question
would issue from the elite of the scientists, perhaps particularly from the
Royal Society. It comes as something of a surprise to find that emancipation from witchcraft beliefs was not included in the extensive catalogue of
benefits to civilisation announced by contemporary apologists for the
Royal Society. Why was this opportunity to promote the interests of sci-

ence missed in a field where the new science appeared to offer such a decisive contribution?

It is unlikely that this issue was carelessly overlooked; the omission of this propaganda weapon is more probably the result of conscious policy than an oversight. The reason lies in the ambiguity of the response to the mechanical philosophy among English natural philosophers. Notwithstanding their early interest in the ideas of Descartes and his associates, and general displays of uninhibited enthusiasm for the new philosophy, they very quickly became alerted to the materialistic dangers of the mechanical philosophy, which in the writings of Thomas Hobbes seemed to be exemplified in its most pernicious form. It was therefore hazardous for the scientific community to pursue mechanism rigorously, and more prudent to adopt the mechanical philosophy in an attenuated form, even at the cost of philosophical untidiness or inconsistency.

There was little departure from the line expressed with lucid gravamen by Sir Thomas Browne, who was alarmed

> how so many learned hands should so far forget their metaphysicks, and destroy the ladder and scale of creatures, as to question the existence of spirits; for my part, I have ever believed, and do now know, that there are witches. They that doubt of these do not only deny them, but spirits: and are obliquely, and upon consequence, a sort, not of infidels, but atheists.[52]

This same message was propagated by the Cambridge Platonists, and it was thoroughly absorbed by the founders of the Royal Society (see illustrations 17 and 18, pp. 90 and 91).

Burton's monumental *Anatomy of Melancholy* (1621; third edition, 1638) devoted one of its longest 'Digressions' to the subject of 'Spirits', as a prelude to demonstrating that the bulk of informed opinion supported the witchcraft idea. This discussion overlapped with his longest Digression, 'Of Air', which also raised the question of intelligences, but in the cosmological context. These subjects were primary interests of Burton, who provided the English reader with a rambling but thoroughly comprehensive and up-to-date review of ancient and modern opinion concerning demonic magic.[53]

Neoplatonic demonology embraced the idea of infinite worlds, each being governed by its own particular pattern of intelligences. The planets themselves were thought to be ruled by olympian spirits of some kind. The animistic conceptions of the earth, moon, planets, and stars evolved by Bruno, Patrizi, Gilbert and Kepler were not entirely free from ideas concerning intelligences. The earth and other planetary bodies were not merely regarded as sharing some diffuse force characterized as the *anima mundi*, but were also thought to possess a complete organic constitution

Recogitabo omnes annos in
amaritudine animæ meæ.
Tu autem eruisti animam me-
am ve non perret, proiecisti.
post tergum tuum,
omnia peccata
mea. Isa. 38.

Ioan. Sradan. invent.

Carol. de Mallery sculp.   Phls Galle excud.

Angelicis plene doctus sermonibus æger   Collocat in Christo spem confirmatus
Et Divûm exemplis, Cœlumq; Erebumq; tuetur: Qui generi humano Servator et anchora sacr

Corn. Kil. Duffl

17. *Ars Moriendi*, engraving by Carel de Mallerii.

marum ins̃tituit, *sacris munítque Sacerdos*:
ngeli ab ætherio veniunt properanter Olympo,

Ads̃tant languenti, lachrymas celantíq̃ Parentum,
Et fugere extemplo Cacodæmonis agmina cogunt.

Corn. Ks͞c. Duffl.

Ars Moriendi, engraving by Carel de Mallerii.

analogous to the human body. The planetary body was revitalized by the circulation of its physiological fluids. Harvey proposed an analogous function for the circulation of blood which he had demonstrated in animals. Just as the earth was thought to gain sustenance from the vital heat at its centre, so Harvey's blood was revitalized in the heart. When seeking an appropriate image to explain this revitalization Harvey fell back on the *lar familiaris*, or household deity, of the ancients.

With the benefit of the closer observation made possible by their newly invented telescopes, astronomers were impressed by similarities between planets and the earth. The force of analogy suggested that planets might be inhabited, immediately suggesting to Burton that Kepler's speculations concerning 'Saturnine and Jovial inhabitants', themselves an echo of Paracelsus and Brahe on *penates,* were in line with the ideas of Proclus and Iamblicus concerning 'the middle betwixt God and men, principalities and princes, which commanded and swayed kings and courtiers, and had several places in the spheres perhaps, for as every sphere is higher, so hath it more excellent inhabitants'. Perhaps better than he knew, Burton detected that the speculations concerning the plurality of worlds which in some sense or other became pervasive among Copernicans, Cartesians, and Newtonians, were not merely based on the principle of scientific analogy, but were also bound up with the Neoplatonic doctrines of divine plenitude and hierarchy.[54] As in the case of the scientific justification of witchcraft, plurality of worlds served to reinject an element of the spiritual into the new cosmology.

Faced with the dilemma of reconciling scientific credibility with religious orthodoxy, adepts of the new science approached the questions of spiritual phenomena and witchcraft in a manner consistent with their attitude towards astrology. They abandoned the purely literary approach of Burton in favour of the study of witchcraft and spirit phenomena with a view to deleting the mass of poorly authenticated stories, and leaving a residuum which could not admit explanation by other than supernatural means. There was clearly lacking by this stage any sense among the scientists that witchcraft posed a great social danger. They approached the problem in the ethos of latterday scientific devotees of spiritualism, hoping that the labour of sorting through bizarre ghost stories would in some way confirm the existence of hierarchies of immortal spirits. But this enterprise as it was conducted can hardly be construed as reinforcing the sceptical position, and to a limited degree it became an adjunct to the renewal of witch-hunting.

The wave of interest in witchcraft and sorcery among the experimental philosophers began with the publication at Robert Boyle's behest of *The Devil of Mascon* (1658). This old story emanating from a reformed minister from the Jura, had for long captured Boyle's interest, and it proved just as successful with other readers, five editions being called for between 1658 and 1679.[55] The devil of Mascon became the anchor man of subsequent compilations of authentic accounts of demons. Boyle continued to believe that the verification of supernatural phenomena represented the best means of invalidating the arguments of atheists.[56] The 'sceptical chymist' and his friends expressed no obvious reservations concerning witchcraft.

Boyle's demonology reflects traditional ideas on divine plenitude. He quoted Grotius on the Jewish idea that earth and heaven were full of spirits: 'And it seems not very likely, that while our terraqueous globe, and our air, are frequented by multitudes of spirits, all the celestial globes . . . and all the aetherial or fluid part of the world should be destitute of inhabitants'. God had created in all realms 'an inestimable multitude of spiritual beings, of various kinds, each of them endowed with an intellect and will of its own', filling the 'distance betwixt the infinite creator and the creatures'.[57] Boyle's cause was particularly energetically pursued by Joseph Glanvill, who together with Thomas Sprat, was the major apologist for the Royal Society. Glanvill even proposed to the influential William, Lord Brereton, that the Society should compile a Baconian Natural History of the 'Land of Spirits'.[58] Individual initiative more than made up for the lack of formal commitment of the Society to this project. Some of the investigations led to negative conclusions: after meticulous investigation Robert Plot decided that fairy rings were unlikely to have been caused by the dancing of witches and their familiars, and he denied the existence of the 'non-Adamical Men' of Paracelsus. But he remained convinced that 'Bad as well as good Angels may be the Ministring spirits and converse with Mankind', and discussed this proposition at length.[59]

Glanvill himself came to devote his major literary energies to the question of witchcraft, his first major statement on the issue being dedicated to Robert Hunt, the Somerset JP, who was zealous in his persecution of witches. Hunt's papers were placed at Glanvill's disposal. Owing to Glanvill's labours the demon of Tedworth and the drummer of Mompesson joined the devil of Mascon as classics of their *genre*. Glanvill was profoundly relieved when rumours that Boyle and Mompesson had come to regard their respective stories as frauds were vigorously denied by these two important authorities.[60] When Glanvill died before completing yet another new edition of his *Saducismus Triumphatus*, this work was taken up by Henry More, whose own early writings had formed the substantial basis for much of the effort of Glanvill and his associates within the Royal Society. There was no lack of helpers, new stories being provided, or the interchange of information being facilitated, by such illustrious names as

19.   Comenius, *Orbis pictus*, 'Providentia dei'.

John Wilkins, Edward Reynolds, or Ralph Cudworth, leading natural philosopher divines of their age.[61]

Saducismus Triumphatus cannot be dismissed as the last feeble manifestation of a dying tradition. Kittredge, with some justice, argued that this attempt to place witchcraft on an unshakable scientific basis exercised more influence than any other English work in its field.[62] On this issue at least the Royal Society was not at odds with its critics. The conservative Meric Casaubon combined attacks on the new philosophy (from which Boyle was exempted), with his own rambling discourses against enthusiasts, whom he regarded as agents of the Devil.[63] The year after the publication of the *Devil of Mascon* Casaubon produced the most notorious of all the 'proofs' of the existence of spirits, his edition of *A True and Faithful Relation of What Passed Between Dr. J. Dee and Some Spirits*, a work which the tortured intellect of Casaubon hoped would stand out as the ultimate example of a 'man deluded: here is frequent preaching and praysing of spirits (reall Divells)'.[64] A writer of greater insight and imagination than Casaubon might have realized that such a clumsy and oblique

20.   Frontispiece from Joseph Glanvill, *Saducismus Triumphatus*.

weapon would immediately arouse suspicion of his involvement in the very movements which he was seeking to discredit.

It is apparent that on the question of witchcraft and sorcery the attitudes of the scientific *avant garde* and their conservative opponents largely coalesced. Each group believed that its own standpoint was the surest protection against atheism and the best grounds for the authority of the established church. Neither party saw advantage in promoting scepticism towards witchcraft beliefs as such. Paradoxically, we find circumstantial evidence suggesting the waning of concern about witchcraft among the elite but very little explicit defence of the sceptical position. Scot's *Discovery of Witchcraft* was reissued in 1665, to be immediately assailed by the authority of 'A Member of the Royal Society', given in place of Glanvill's name on the title-page of his *Philosophical Endeavour towards the Defence of the Being of Witches and Apparitions* (1666). This work appeared in four different editions, and some dozen different printings before 1700, completely swamping any literary effort of the sceptics.

Opposition to the Royal Society on the question of witchcraft must have seemed feeble: for instance John Wagstaffe, an obscure Fellow of Oriel College, was thought to be the author of a mischievous pamphlet directed against Wilkins and Wallis and their Experimental Philosophy Club at Oxford, shortly before this group moved to London to found the Royal Society. Wagstaffe incautiously drew upon the arguments of Hobbes, himself polemicist against Wallis and Boyle, and no friend of the Royal Society. Wagstaffe was ridiculed for his work and on account of his dwarfish appearance.[65]

The only substantial response to the work of Glanvill emanated from John Webster, the celebrated enthusiast preacher physician who had led the radicals' attack on universities during the Revolution and so provoked a torrent of response from the puritan establishment led by Wilkins and Ward. Since the restoration Webster had led a retiring existence as a medical practitioner in Clitheroe, an area well-known for witchcraft. His work shed its earlier polemical flavour and he wrote two major books in the manner of a learned physician, the first, as already mentioned, on metallurgy, and the second *The Displaying of Witchcraft* (1677). Webster clearly hoped that his work would appeal to the Royal Society, and in the case of the book on witchcraft he secured the *imprimatur* of Sir Jonas Moore the Vice-President of the Society, probably because of the latter's origins and continuing connections with intellectuals in the Pendle area. This seeming concession by the Royal Society to the sceptics caused acute annoyance to Glanvill. Webster's work is evidently the result of deep reflection, and it is clear that he had been collecting notes on witchcraft for some considerable time. No doubt his outlook had been determined during the Republic when his own writings must have contributed to eliciting attempts by More, Casaubon, and others to make the connection between religious enthusiasm and witchcraft.

One defence of the sectarian position was denial of the existence of evil intelligences, or at least severe limitation of their powers to intervene in nature. The former course was taken by Lodowick Muggleton, and the latter by John Webster. Authentic local knowledge, widespread experience in medical practice, extensive reading in medical sources, and longstanding sympathy with Paracelsianism, equipped Webster for a far-ranging and convincing defence of the sceptical position, scarcely deserving the poor press received from modern commentators. The main failing is the ponderous scholastic structure adapted for the purpose of impressing the university scholars, which is only occasionally allowed to give way to shafts of trenchant prose of the kind which typified his earlier sermons.

There was very little in Webster's exposition which would have been unfamiliar to contemporaries of Weyer. Witchcraft phenomena were explained partly by natural magic, partly by delusion. It was repeatedly denied that devils 'appear to Witches in the shape of Cats, Dogs, Squirrels or the like, to the end to suck upon their bodies or to have carnal copulation with them, or to transport them in the air to places far distant, to dance, revel, feast and to do homage to the Devil . . . for so impure, filthy, horrid and abominable ends'.[66] Natural magic is invoked to explain many of the phenomena associated with witchcraft, much of the explanation assuming the language of contemporary atomism.

But in the end, like his sixteenth-century precursors, and colleagues in the Royal Society, Webster is convinced by the authority of the scriptures that he cannot deny the existence 'of Spirits either good or bad, nor utterly overthrow the truth of apparitions'.[67] Neither was it denied that these intelligences would exert physical effects. Webster was more conversant with the most modern physiological writings than most other English writers on witchcraft. He could find nothing in these writings to controvert Paracelsus' idea of the astral spirit which was the basis of the latter's explanation of apparitions. Given this concession, Webster quickly came to accept the devil of Mascon and much else of its kind, so greatly narrowing the distance between himself and the Fellows of the Royal Society, and preparing the ground for infinite regress on the question of witchcraft beliefs.

The risks of undertaking a more determined assault on the spirit world than that attempted by Webster are indicated by the fate of Balthasar Bekker in the Netherlands, whose *World Bewitch'd* (1695, from Dutch edition 1691) was met by savage criticism from the religious establishment. Bekker was attacked as a Cartesian, Hobbist, and Spinozan atheist. Significantly, the major reply to Bekker, from Jacob Koelman, drew heavily from Glanvill and More.[68]

Webster, like Weyer before him, left too many loopholes to provide a totally convincing case against witchcraft. Demons remained a part of the worldview of the English intelligentsia and there is no indication that the position changed in the last decades of the century. The dominance of traditional lore is evident from the review of the question of spirits produced by John Beaumont, who was not an obscure backwoodsman, but a capable geologist, leading light of the Somerset Philosophical Society, and contributor to the theory of the earth debate. Beaumont's voluminous *An Historical, Physiological and Theological Treatise of Spirits* (1705) indicates that comprehensive acquaintance with ancient and Renaissance Neoplatonic sources was not a thing of the past. Paracelsus was cited at length on the capacity of the sidereal spirit to part company with the body.

Beaumont had little to add to the fund of local stories concerning spirits, but he firmly maintained that well-authenticated stories should be accepted, and he was unwilling to discount stories of witchcraft. He believed that Le Clerc and Cudworth had convincingly answered philosophers like Locke who threw doubt on the idea of spiritual substance.[69] Whiston firmly supported Beaumont's point of view, using the evidence of scriptural sources. He associated the Devil with meteors, and believed that this was a means whereby demons caused pestilence and famine. The ubiquity and power of demons he thought were as firmly attested as Boyle's experiments on the elasticity of air, or Newton's demonstrations of the power of gravity.[70]

Whiston's defence of witchcraft was dictated by important matters of principle. The power of demons, he believed, was a necessary condition for the acceptance of Divine Providence. He was shocked that some of his contemporaries were questioning 'the imposition of good Angels, or wicked Demons in the Affairs of this World; yet which has been the constant Opinion, or rather Experience and Attestation of all Mankind, excepting the Sadducees and Epicureans, in all the past Ages of the World, till the present Age'.[71] To Whiston, demons were just as necessary for the concept of Providence as eclipses, comets, northern lights, meteors, and earthquakes. Any purely naturalistic explanation of these phenomena would detract from the idea of the extraordinary powers of God, and thereby cast doubt on the entire scheme of universal history.

In particular the climactic phase of the eschatological sequence would involve the particularly active intervention of the Devil, as the elect wrestled with agents of Antichrist. Whiston considered that Flamsteed and Locke were essentially on his side, by virtue of the former's conceding the power of Providence in the genesis of earthquakes, and the latter's accepting that miracles in the Old Testament might originate from either God or the Devil. Newton's own instincts were in the same direction, his apparent adoption of a mechanical solution of gravity being forced on him by John Machin against his 'declar'd Sense of his own Mind over many Years together'. Newton allowed himself to be driven to this 'absurd' position because of some fear of attributing things to demons or invisible beings.[72] Whiston argued that it was he rather than Newton who represented the position of such standard-bearers as Cudworth, Le Clerc and Limborch against Spinozism, by insisting that belief in the occurrence of miracles beyond the period of the Testaments was essential support for the idea that a power above nature was continually in operation.[73]

It is a tenacious tradition dating back to the time of Richard Bentley's Boyle lectures and extending to Lecky and present-day histories, that the new science and its agents, the distinguished Fellows of the Royal Society, played a major part in the decline of witchcraft beliefs in Britain.[74] Primary responsibility for this idea was assumed by Francis Hutchinson, the first historian of witchcraft in England, who boasted that England was 'the first that purg'd itself from these deep Superstitions . . . as our Nation wards explaining how the Royal Society had effected its enlightening purpose in the field of witchcraft belief, not even the suggestion that adoption of the mechanical philosophy was incompatible with belief in witch-our Witchcraft have been banish'd, but all Arts and Sciences have been greatly improv'd'.[75] Hutchinson however offered no further grounds towards explaining how the Royal Society had effected its enlightening purpose in the field of witchcraft belief, not even the suggestion that adoption of the mechanical philosophy was incompatible with belief in witchcraft. Closer examination of Hutchinson's book suggests that this issue was consciously avoided. All the indications are that he was by no means confident that his views coincided with informed opinion among his contemporaries.

The then obscure clergyman of Bury St Edmunds did not improve the clarity of his argument by using a dialogue form. He estimated that of the twenty-four books devoted to his subject since 1660 none had adopted his position. John Aubrey was mentioned as an author on the other side. Had Hutchinson investigated more closely it would have emerged that a substantial portion of the literature favourable to witchcraft belief was contributed by Glanvill, Aubrey and other writers having firm associations with the Royal Society.

As indicated above, there is very little evidence of direct or indirect kind to support the view of Hutchinson, and much to suggest that the ethos of the new science was best preserved by taking up a conservative stance on the question of witchcraft and sorcery. This issue provided the

Royal Society with an opportunity of demonstrating its religious and social conformity and freedom from suspected materialistic leanings. The only major critique of this position emanated, as we have seen, from a retired revolutionary and enthusiast who was a devotee of Paracelsus.

It is clear moreover that the position of members of the Royal Society with respect to demonic magic was adopted from conviction rather than prudence. A demonic dimension to divine plenitude and the warfare between the forces of good and evil were consistent with the prevailing idea of Providence. To the degree that attitudes in general were changing about such questions as witchcraft persecution, scientists were dragged along with the tide. We must look in places other than science for the explanation of these changes.

The witchcraft case history draws attention to the degree to which our ideas concerning the broader relevance of the Scientific Revolution are still conditioned by the positivistic framework bequeathed by the generation of Lecky. The closer study of prophecy, spiritual magic, and demonic magic suggests correctives to some sweeping generalizations relating to the nature and impact of the modern scientific movement. During the last decades we have gained a much clearer idea of the course of scientific innovation. Descriptive elements of the worldview are well understood. But this is only a partial contribution towards the understanding of the outlook of an age in which questions of science and religion were inseparable.

NOTES

1. R.H. Robbins, *The Encyclopaedia of Witchcraft and Demonology* (New York, 1960); J.B. Russell, *Witchcraft in the Middle Ages* (Ithaca, N.Y., 1972).

2. J. Hansen, *Quellen und Untersuchungen zur Geschichte des Herenwahns und der Herenverfolgung im Mittelalter* (Bonn, 1901), pp.38–42; H.C. Lea, *Materials toward a History of Witchcraft*, ed. A.C. Howland, 3 vols (Philadelphia, 1939), **1**, 178–80; J.T. McNeil and H.M. Gamer, *Medieval Handbooks of Penance* (New York, 1938), pp.32–5.

3. Psellus, as represented in such collective works as Iamblicus of Chalcis, *De mysteriis Aegyptiorum* (Lyons, 1549), pp.338–40; G. Pictorius, *Pantapolion . . . de daemonum* (Basel, 1562/3), 'De illorum daemonum', pp.14–15, 24. Bodin, *Démonomanie des Sorciers* (Paris, 1580), fol.105.

4. For general background to Neoplatonic demonology, see H. Ritter and M. Plessner (1962), *Das Ziel des Weisen von Pseudo-Maǧrītī, Studies of the Warburg Institute*, vol. **27**; G. Soury, *La Demonologie de Plutarque* (Paris, 1942); R. Müller-Sternberg, *Die Dämonen, Wesen und Ursprung eines Urphänomens* (Bremen, 1964); J. Kroll, *Die Lehren des Hermes Trismegistus* (Münster, 1914); Walker, *Spiritual and Demonic Magic*; W.C. van Dam, *Dämonen und besessene* (Aschaffenburg, 1970).

5. Trithemius, *Antipalus maleficiorum* and *Liber octo quaestionum*, both dating from 1508; K. Arnold, *Johannes Trithemius* (Würzburg, 1971); *idem* (1975), Additamenta Trithemiana . . . *De demonibus*, *Würzburger Diözesan-Geschichtsblätter*, **37/38**, 239–67.

6. Champier, *Dialogus in magicarum artium* (Lyons, 1500), II, 3, in B. Copenhaver, *Symphorien Champier* (The Hague, 1978), pp.191–7.

7. Agrippa, *De vanitate scientiarum* (Antwerp, 1530), chapters 44, 45, 48, 96; *Opera*, **1**, 71–6, 80–2, 218–21. P. Zambelli (1972), Cornelio Agrippa, Sisto da Siena e gli Inquisitori, in Motivi di riformi tra '400 e '500, *Memorie domenicane*, n.s. **3**, 146–64.

8. Agricola, *Bermannus sive de re metallica dialogus* (Basel, 1530), p.38; *Ausgewählte Werke*, ed. H. Prescher, 12 vols (Berlin, 1955-), **2**, 88. *Idem, De animantibus subterraneis liber* (Basel, 1549), pp.77–8; *Ausgewählte Werke*, **6**, 200.

9. H.C. Erik Midelfort, *Witch Hunting in Southwestern Germany 1562–1684* (Stanford, California, 1972), pp.36–56; H.A. Oberman, *Masters of the Reformation: The Emergence of a New Intellectual Climate in Europe*, transl. D. Martin (Cambridge, 1981), pp.158–83.

10. C. Zilboorg and G.W. Henry, *A History of Medical Psychology* (New York, 1941), pp.195–200; C. Zilboorg, *The Medical Man and the Witch During the Renaissance* (Baltimore, 1935); I. Galdston, The Psychiatry of Paracelsus in *Psychiatry and the Human Condition* (New York, 1976), pp.337–89. For the most detailed review, an odd mixture of ancient and modern: M. Jacob (1959), Die Hexenlehre des Paracelsus und ihre Bedeutung für die Modernen Hexenprozesse (unpublished Ph.D. dissertation, Erlangen).

11. *Von den unsichtbaren Krankheiten*, PI, **9**, 258,309; *Elf Tractat*, PI, **1**, 137.

12. *Astronomia Magna*, PI, **12**, 276–85, 369–402.

13. *De occulta philosophia*, PI, **14**, 532–4.

14. *De occulta philosophia*, PI, **14**, 515–16.

15. *Von den unsichtbaren Krankheiten*, PI, **9**, 325–6.

16. *Volumen Paramirum*, PI, **1**, 215–24.

17. *De occulta philosophia*, PI, **14**, 532–4.

18. *Liber artis praesagis*, PI, **14**, 21; *Astronomia Magna*, PI, **12**, 86–8; *De virtute imaginativa*, PI, **14**, 313.

19. *De meteoris*, PI, **13**, 271–5; *Liber artis praesagis*, PI, **14**, 14–18.

20. *Von den unsichtbaren Krankheiten*, PI, **9**, 291.

21. *De peste*, PI, **9**, 597; *De pestilitate*, PI, **14**, 649.

22. *De occulta philosophia*, PI, **14**, 535–6; *Volumen Paramirum*, PI, **1**, 221.

23. *Von den unsichtbaren Krankheiten*, PI, **9**, 346–7.

24. *Liber artis praesagis*, PI, **14**, 21–2.

25. *De occulta philosophia*, PI, **14**, 514–16, 536–42.

26. *De occulta philosophia*, PI, **14**, 538–9.

27. *De occulta philosophia*, PI, **14**, 516–19; *Volumen Paramirum*, PI, **1**, 215–33.

28. *De occulta philosophia*, PI, **14**, 541.

29. *Liber artis praesagis*, PI, **14**, 25–7.

30. *Von den unsichtbaren Krankheiten*, PI, **9**, 300–2; *Liber artis praesagis*, PI, **14**, 23–4, 26–7.

31. *De nymphis*, PI, **14**, 141–3.

32. *De occulta philosophia*, PI, **14**, 323–4.

33. *Von den unsichtbaren Krankheiten*, PI, **9**, 323–4; *Liber artis praesagis*, PI, **14**, 8–9.

34. *Volumen Paramirum*, PI, **1**, 207.

35. *Von den unsichtbaren Krankheiten*, PI, **9**, 297–303.

36. *Liber artis praesagis*, PI, **14**, 26–7.

37. *De nymphis*, PI, **14**, 123–4. Sir Thomas Browne, *Pseudodoxia Epidemica*, IV, 11, ed. R. Robbins, 2 vols (Oxford, 1981), **1**, 332–3.

38. *De occulta philosophia*, PI, **14**, 526.

39. *De morbis amentium*, PI, **2**, 420–6.

40. Brahe, *Opera Omnia*, **2**, 207; see also **1**, 166–7.

41. For example, Zilboorg and Henry, *History of Medical Psychology*, pp.207–35; Zilboorg, *The Medical Man and the Witch*.

42. Midelfort, *Witch Hunting in Southwestern Germany*, pp.25–6.

43. K. Sprengel, *Histoire de la Médicine*, transl. A.J.L. Jourdan, 9 vols (Paris, 1815–20), **3**, 233–6. S. Anglo, Melancholia and witchcraft: the debate between Wier, Bodin and Scot, in A. Gerlo, ed., *Folie et Déraison à la Renaissance* (Brussels, 1976), pp.209–22; C. Baxter, Johann Weyer's *De Praestigiis Daemonum:* unsystematic psychopathology, in S. Anglo, ed., *The Damned Art* (London, 1977), pp.53–75.

44. Anglo, pp.209–21; Thomas, *Religion and the Decline of Magic*, p.579.

45. William Perkins, *Discourse of the Damned Art of Witchcraft* (Cambridge, 1608), pp.190–4.

46. John Cotta, *A Short Discoverie of the Unobserved Dangers of Severall Sorts of Ignorant and Unconsiderate Practisers of Physicke in England* (London, 1612), p.58.

47. Stephen Bredwell, Marie Glovers late woefull case, British Library, Sloane MS 831; Edward Jorden, *A Brief Discourse of the Suffocation of the Mother* (London, 1603). Discussed briefly in R. Hunter and I. Macalpine, *Three Hundred Years of Psychiatry 1535–1860* (London, 1963), pp.68–75; Thomas, *Religion and the Decline of Magic*, pp.511, 537, 546, 558; J. Boss (1979), The seventeenth century transformation of the hysteric affection, *Psychological Medicine*, **9**, 221–34; Sir G. Clark, *A History of the Royal College of Physicians of London*, 2 vols (Oxford, 1964–6), **1**, 168; D.P. Walker, *Unclean Spirits: Possession and Exorcism in France and England in the late Sixteenth and early Seventeenth Centuries* (Philadelphia, 1981), pp.79–80.

48. Howell to Sir Edward Spencer, 20 February 1647, *Epistolae Ho-Elianae* (1645–7), ed. J. Jacobs, 2 vols (London, 1890–2), **2**, 547–51.

49. Robert Burton, *The Anatomy of Melancholy*, 3 vols (Everyman edn), **1**, 192.

50. Edward Poeton, The winnowing of white witchcraft, British Library, Sloane MS 1954, f.4v.

51. Webster, *Displaying of Witchcraft*, pp.323–4.

52. Browne, *Religio Medici*, I, 30.

53. Burton, *Anatomy*, 1, 180–206; 2, 34–69.

54. Burton, *Anatomy*, 1, 51–6. For recent reviews, see P. Rossi, Nobility of Man and Plurality of Worlds in Debus, ed., *Science, Medicine and Society*, 2, 130–62; S.J.Dick (1980), The origins of the extraterrestrial life debate and its relation to the scientific revolution, *Journal of the History of Ideas*, 41, 3–27.

55. E. Labrousse, Le Démon de Mâcon, in Istituto Nazionale di Studi sul Rinascimento, *Scienze, Credenze Occulte Livelli di Cultura* (Florence, 1982), pp.249–75.

56. Boyle to Glanvill, 18 September 1677, *Works*, 6, 57–8.

57. Boyle (1685), Of the high veneration man's intellect owes to God, in *Works*, 5, 146–8. See also Excellency of theology (1674), *Works*, 4, 19.

58. Glanvill, *A Blow at Modern Sadducism* (London, 1668), pp.115–17. This proposal seems not to be included in other editions. M.E. Prior (1932), Joseph Glanvill, witchcraft and seventeenth century science, *Modern Philology*, 30, 167–93.

59. Plot, *Staffordshire*, pp.9–19. For a further much-discussed subject: witchcraft and butter-making, see Beale to Boyle, 28 April 1666, *Works*, 6, 400–1. See illustration 19, p.94.

60. Boyle to Glanvill, 10 February 1677/8, *Works*, 6, 59–60.

61. Other helpers of Glanvill included Boyle's brother the Earl of Orrery, the Earl of Lauderdale, and Sir George Mackenzie. See illustration 20, p.95.

62. G.L. Kittredge, *Witchcraft in Old and New England* (Cambridge, Mass., 1929), p.335.

63. Casaubon was also a friend of Paul du Moulin, the translator of *The Devil of Mascon*.

64. M.R.G. Spiller, *'Concerning Natural Experimental Philosophie': Meric Casaubon and the Royal Society* (The Hague, 1980), p.8.

65. A. Wood, *Athenae Oxonienses*, ed. P. Bliss, 4 vols (Oxford, 1813–20), 3, 1113–14.

66. Webster, *Displaying of Witchcraft*, p.229.

67. *Displaying*, p.293.

68. R.L. Colie, *Light and Enlightenment: A Study of the Cambridge Platonists and the Dutch Arminians* (Cambridge, 1957), pp.105–7.

69. Beaumont, *An Historical Treatise*, p.337.

70. Whiston, *An Account of the Daemoniacks and of the Power of Casting Out Daemons* (London, 1737), pp.71, 74–5.

71 Whiston, *Memoirs*, 2, 120.

72. Whiston, *Memoirs*, 2, 190–8.

73. Colie, *Light and Enlightenment*, pp.107–11.

74. Richard Bentley, *Remarks upon a Late Discourse of Free Thinking* (London, 1713), p.33. W.E.H. Lecky, *History of the Rise and Influence of Rationalism in Europe* (London, 1865; 2 vols, 1910 edn), 1, 109–10.

75. F. Hutchinson, *An Historical Essay Concerning Witchcraft* (London, 1718), pp.33–5.

INDEX